Don't Bank on It!

Be prepared for what may well be the most valuable book you will read this year and for years to come.

Now, after five more years of research, money-management expert Martin J. Meyer reveals astonishing new techniques for tripling and even quadrupling your interest on your savings—all fully insured.

Each chapter of this remarkable book is a gold mine of profitable information and startling disclosures that not only reveal ingenious ways to multiply your savings, but teach you the *methodology* of astute savings and investments. With the knowledge you gain from Meyer's disclosures, you will know what to look for to achieve maximum interest and safety for your money. And you will also know what to avoid.

DON'T BANK ON IT!

How To Make Up To 22%
Or More On Your Savings—
All Fully Insured

by

Martin J. Meyer

PUBLISHED BY POCKET BOOKS NEW YORK

POCKET BOOKS, a Simon & Schuster division of
GULF & WESTERN CORPORATION
1230 Avenue of the Americas, New York, N.Y. 10020

Published by arrangement with Farnsworth Publishing Company, Inc.
Library of Congress Catalog Card Number: 79-3156

ISBN: 0-671-41606-5

First Pocket Books printing November, 1980

10 9 8 7 6 5 4 3 2 1

POCKET and colophon are trademarks of Simon & Schuster.

Printed in the U.S.A.

Dedication

To the average American,
whose standard of living and
financial security are now threatened,
this book is dedicated.

Acknowledgments

I am indebted to Gene Hessler of the Photographic Department of the Chase Manhattan Bank for his successful efforts in locating pictures of old coins and currency.

My thanks for the friendly cooperation of John J. Toolan and Kathy Abravaya of the Great Neck Office of Chase.

To Lee Rosler of Farnsworth Publishing, my gratitude for his patience.

Preface

Do you know how it feels to have an estate worth a million dollars? Or even a quarter-million?

Probably not.

Yet you can not only know how it feels, *you can have it—* even if you are now in debt, with liabilities exceeding your assets.

Very few people in our society can boast of substantial net worth. A few inherit it, win it in lotteries, at the track, in the stock market, or in casinos.

Others—such as doctors, lawyers, successful business persons, top athletes, big corporate executives, and entertainers— earn enough to amass it.

But those who do have the wealth are usually too busy making and enjoying it to have the time to preserve it. So, for each one who has it, there are 10 others working night and day to take it away. All too often the wealthy person is lured by stocks, warrants, commodity futures, puts and calls, land, tax shelters, and dozens of other schemes which offer a great deal for little and, too frequently, give nothing in return.

On the other hand, most of us weren't born into wealth, won't strike a bonanza, and will never earn it.

How then can the young man or woman, with average or slightly better income, build an estate of a million dollars—or at least a quarter-million? It *can* be done without risk or hard work. All it takes is motivation and knowledge.

Many readers of this book will already have put aside some

"nest-egg" against that worrisome "rainy day" that can occur to anyone at any time. What this book will do is teach them not only how to add to this cache, but also, *more* importantly, how to make it grow 10 or 15 fold.

Others may have some net worth (equity in a home, automobile, or furniture) but minimal liquid assets (cash and bank accounts readily convertible into currency). *Now* is the time for *them* to start building an estate. Some may owe more than they have. Like it or not, the lure of credit has plunged more than half of this nation's families into that unenviable position. Their debts to banks, finance companies, credit cards, chain and department stores amount to more than the sum of all they possess. What they learn here could prove to be their life raft in a troubled financial sea. But—fair warning—those who are heavily in debt will need more than a desire; they must have the *will* to succeed.

To repeat, what can be learned here will make it possible for anyone with average intelligence, income, health, and future productivity expectancy to build an estate of hundreds of thousands of dollars. But it won't happen without some effort on your part. The more thoroughly you learn and the more closely you follow the recommendations, the greater the wealth you shall amass.

Why should you believe this promise? Isn't it true that, as one savings bank ad says, the only ones who profit from "get-rich-quick" books are the ones who write them?

In answer to the first question, the reliability of a promise is best established through the qualifications and credibility of its maker. Traditionally, the place for a writer's biographical blurb is the book jacket. But you are entitled to more; you should know enough about the author to start with some confidence in him and in the validity of his claims. The book *itself* can then convince you.

As to the second question: Does the author of "get-rich-quick" books make a pile of money from them?

Yes. If he or she is lucky enough to be the one in a thousand whose book takes off because it's got something unique and concrete to offer and captures the public's imagination.

The first edition of DON'T BANK ON IT!, published in 1970, was just such a book. Hugely successful, it has been referred to by banking establishment sources as the prime motivator for many of the recent changes in banking regulations.

But bureaucracies move slowly and ineffectually—when they move at all. One of the purposes of this new edition is to show you how to use the new regulations to profit even more substantially than was possible under the old rules. After all, the idea of a "new edition" is to keep one abreast of the times!

But, as regards my credibility, my recent success should not be all upon which you base your judgment. It is the *past* which should be your portent to the future. Here, then, are the facts.

Born in 1921 into an educated middle class family, I enjoyed the post-World War I prosperity until my father was struck down by a long illness, and the great depression lowered the boom.

With a near-genius I.Q., I received my secondary education at a small, free, city run, college-preparatory school for the "intellectual elite," from which a predominance of students eventually became doctors, lawyers, professors, corporation presidents, and Nobel Prize winners.

But not me.

Graduated before my fifteenth birthday but unable to accept the Ivy League scholarships which I was offered, I worked evenings to help keep food on the table and a roof over the family's head. Attending the local City College, I concentrated on the pure sciences—chemistry, physics, and math. Post-graduate professional schools were out of the question; earning a living took top priority.

For several years, from age 19 on, I worked as an Army Ordinance engineer, designing and developing methods for the mass production of ammunition, a responsibility I shared with a handful of much older men. When our military victory in World War II was evident, I was lured into private industry. While taking a short break before starting on the new job, I learned my first lesson in personal economics: After over three years of steady work as a professional employee, I was in debt—for $75. After three and a half years, seven and a half percent of my productive life, I had less than nothing to show for it.

After my short stint in the private sector, with borrowed money, a fellow employee and I struck out on our own. In short order our fledgling consulting engineering venture counted many of the blue-chip industrials among its clients, and a staff of professionals and support personnel numbering over a hundred. To maintain quality and satisfy delivery requirements for research and technical reports, we even built our own plant for printing, photography, processing, plate making, and binding.

But after 18 years I grew bored with my life as an entrepreneur. I had reached the conclusion that I wasn't using my knowledge and talents to anywhere near their fullest extent. Unfortunately, a restrictive partnership agreement prevented me from selling my shares in the business. To quit, I had to walk away. I did. At age 41.

Though not poor, I didn't retire a rich man for a number of reasons. Profits were invariably used to buy newer, better equipment. During slack periods, in line with our policy not to lay off talented people, employees drew full salary. (Having known hunger during the depression, I could never bring myself to fire a competent worker.) And by industry standards, the employees were well paid—to the extent that no union, including the powerful printers' union, ever came close to winning an NLRB election.

So although I did not get rich from my reputable middle-sized business, I had learned another economic lesson, one seldom voiced or written about: A business can make more money by either charging its customers more or paying its employees less. Since we couldn't do the former—bids were highly competitive—and wouldn't do the latter, my own earnings from the business were not commensurate with my contribution, and not comparable to those of similarly situated business persons or executives. When I left the business, my partner, who had earned the same as I had, was about $20,000 in debt. By comparison, I, the retiring partner, had built an estate of approximately a quarter of a million dollars.

I faced "retirement" with two abiding interests: scientific research, for which I had been trained, and working with money—to make it multiply. Even if I pursued both interests without any certain expectation of financial gain, I could still live indefinitely, I hoped, on the income my estate would provide.

While still in business, I had become interested in money, finance, and banking. Now I was free to expand my knowledge. The movement of money from areas of excess to those of need particularly caught my attention—because a few "money brokers" were apparently earning millions for performing the essential service of moving a half-billion dollars from east to west annually.

Discovering a new aspect of money movement although still a comparatively novice financier, I reviewed my idea with a lawyer friend. We both plunged in headlong, investing $50,000 each. The incentive was there: the potential for earning 18% or more the first year, 25% the following years, with our entire investment returned after two years. Should either of us have need for our capital earlier, it could be retrieved without loss at the end of any calendar quarter. And, most attractive of all, every cent of our investment was guaranteed by U.S. Government agencies!

The idea worked to perfection. In a short time several friends, with whom I had shared the idea, started playing the money-moving game—all dealing with reputable banking institutions including some of the largest in the country. I didn't get rich from the idea, but $50,000 did earn me $9,500 the first year and $12,500 thereafter, with complete safety and liquidity of capital. It was certainly better than the $2,250 a year that $50,000 would have earned in a savings account at the time.

Interestingly, I had recognized this simple, sure, safe method of earning such high interest only because I understood "float" and the principle of credit based on fractional reserves—the very principle upon which the Federal Reserve and our banking systems are built. (See Appendix.) Just as lawyers find loopholes in tax laws, so had I found a loophole in banking practice.

The concept was based on the traditional movement of money from areas which enjoyed an excess of funds to areas which had an insufficient supply. By late 1966, though, *all areas of the country* were credit starved. The gravy-train had lasted until the first "credit crunch" created by the Federal Reserve in its vain attempt to throttle inflation.

Some people play cards, chess, Monopoly. Why not play with real money in the banking system? The knowledgeable, alert person holds a hundred and one trump cards, with opportunities for making additional money unbounded. A bank advertisement in the *New York Times* spurred me to send for details. In short order my friends and I had accounts that paid interest six months at a time—even though money was in the accounts for less than one month out of the six! Money earned double bank interest—85% of the time. Or put another way, while in the account, the principal earned six times normal bank interest.

As the years went by, ways of earning more on capital varied with changes in the economy, banking practice, and interest rates, but there were always dozens of ways to pick up extra dollars—as long as one knew how to spot the ever-recurrent loopholes. The earnings from these money games, supplemented by some of the income from my nest-egg, were enough to live on very comfortably.

Anxious to share my discoveries with others, I decided to write a book describing all of the then-existing methods for earning additional income from the banking system. It was an immediate success. Its title: DON'T BANK ON IT!

A non-fiction, hard-cover book is generally considered a bestseller if 25,000 copies are sold. DON'T BANK ON IT! sold over fifteen times that amount. With periodic updating and revision, the book remained popular for seven years. An auspicious beginning, indeed, for my career as financial author-analyst.

With a highly successful book on banking under my belt, I turned my attention to another area of the finance world rich in opportunities for monetary gain—the credit card industry. My second book, CREDITCARDSMANSHIP, did well enough to merit the publication three years later of a revised edition (titled HOW TO TURN PLASTIC INTO GOLD).

Both books were stimuli for major changes in banking and credit card practice, changes that benefited the consumer. It is interesting to note that *The American Banker,* the publication of the American Bankers Association, had warned the banking industry that DON'T BANK ON IT! would force the payment of higher interest rates to depositors. CREDITCARDSMANSHIP was used as a source book by the attorneys of the Consumers Union of the United States in their successful suit against the major credit card companies.

Though both books have continued to sell, author and publisher agreed that a completely new volume was needed, one that not only explained current methods for increasing earnings on savings, but also taught the reader how to recognize future opportunities and, possibly most important of all, showed how to accumulate the capital base with which to build a respectable estate—even for people who don't have a dime today.

Taking advantage of just one of the many banking and credit card loopholes described in this new edition will earn you back many times the cost of the book. Better yet, you'll learn about banking, its regulatory agencies, interest computation, funds transfer, float, fractional reserve, and elasticity. Though it may be hard to believe, people with this knowledge can and do earn up to two and a half times as much interest on the same amount of money for the same period of time and with the same safety and protection of federal insurance—whether it be for a few days or for thirty or more years. Once you have this knowledge, you will be able to recognize new loopholes that offer extra earnings.

And a lot more is available to you. You'll learn the philosophy of estate building, of creating a capital base. If you really want to be worth hundreds of thousands of dollars, not only can your goal be attained, but you can enjoy a healthier, saner life style, secure in the knowledge that you are prepared for any financial emergency and can look forward to eventual retirement in luxury.

Contents

1.

The Banking System And You

Money is one of the prime movers in life. Its pursuit, possession, and retention is a subject of paramount concern to most responsible citizens.

Long gone are the days of the English goldsmith-banks (see Appendix) and the mattress stuffed with cash. For the vast majority of people today, the preferred institutions for the safeguarding and growth of cash assets are banks. But that is not all. Each of the major types of banking institutions (commercial banks, savings banks, and savings and loan associations) offers many unpublicized opportunities to make *extra* money as well—money well in excess of the advertised interest rates.

Sometimes, the extra dividends will amount to only a few dollars, even a few cents; other times the earnings will total thousands. In some cases, additional income may accrue for but a few days; in others it can continue for decades. Either way, it is money that otherwise would not have been made: "found money." And, if the found money is not frittered away, but rather added to one's savings, that *alone* can make the difference between a meager and a comfortable estate.

One of the most versatile and popular methods of picking up extra money is the exploitation of "float." The dictionary defines (financial) float as "a sum of money representing checks that are outstanding." It is a tradition with a long history. After the Civil War, when paying bills to distant creditors, individuals and businesses often issued checks weeks before the funds to cover those checks were due to be deposited.

This practice was possible because it took several weeks before a mailed check was returned to its bank for payment (by withdrawal of the funds from the account on which the check had been drawn). The "clearance time" of such checks issued was several weeks, and it is this period that is referred to as float.

Conversely, when a check was received from a distant source, it took several weeks for the check to "clear" into the account into which it had been deposited. This extended clearance time, or float, operated to the advantage of the check issuer, but was a liability to the recipient.

Today, float has been shortened, but it is still profitable to the check writer and need not be disadvantageous to the recipient—unless a check bounces. We'll give a number of examples of how float can be used to financial advantage, how some businesses have made as much as a million dollars a year on it, and how a discount can be earned on most bills you pay.

Most business operates with borrowed money—funds borrowed from banks, insurance companies, and in the money markets through issuance of commercial paper. Over the past several years, this financing has incurred an annual cost of from 6% to over 12% of the amount borrowed. Two ways to reduce the amount necessary to be borrowed are first to speed up the receipt of money and, secondly, to slow down the disbursement of money. But customers won't pay their bills to business quicker than they have been paying, nor can business further delay their payments to creditors. Business, however, can accomplish both ends through proper and legal exploitation of float, using methods that banks themselves use.

Business divides float into two parts: clearance float and mail float. For example, a business in New York City receives a $1,500 check from a customer in Sandusky, Ohio, on a Monday. The check is dated and was mailed the previous Wednesday. The sender of the check (to whom float is an asset) considers *mail float* to be from Wednesday to Monday, or five days. If the check clears out of his or her account the following Friday, *clearance float* is from Monday to Friday, or four days. Thus, *total float* as computed by the *sender* is nine days.

The business recipient of the check (to whom float is a liability) likewise considers mail float to be five days, but clearance float to that same recipient may be only two days to a total of seven days— for a reason the reader should be aware of:

> When a member bank remits a received check to its Federal Reserve Bank for clearing, if the check is drawn on another member bank, the bank will be credited with the funds within two days (often one day) after the reserve bank receives the check. Thus, when you deposit to your account any check that you have received, your bank is credited with the amount of the check within two days of their remittance of the check to their reserve bank.

> It is important to take note of a popular misconception promulgated by our highly respected media: that the Federal Reserve System guarantees that the payee can use the funds two days after he or she deposits any check drawn on any member bank. The Fed makes *no such guarantee*. The *bank's* account is credited within two days, but *not necessarily the depositor's account*. Banks often take from four to twenty days to clear a check into an account. Of course, all is fair in love and war—and banking. Favored business accounts can usually arrange to have their banks clear checks within two days.

How this regulation may affect the individual depositor will be discussed in later pages.

The two-day-maximum-clearance Federal Reserve regulation, if helpful to most banks and some check recipients, can also be very costly to other banks. Here is how one major bank decreased its costs by, or made, about $5,000 a day by decreasing its clearance float time by just one day:

> In 1974, when the prime rate was about 12%, the First National Bank in St. Louis realized that every day its customers deposited an average of $15 million in checks that had been drawn on five banks in Chicago. Ordinarily, these and all other checks were sent for clearance to the Federal Reserve Bank in St. Louis, from which the Chicago banks' checks were transferred to the Federal Reserve Bank in Chicago, which, in turn, debited the accounts of the five Chicago banks. The account of the First National Bank was credited two days after the Reserve Bank in St. Louis received the checks.

> First National found that if it didn't use the Fed's clearing system, but rather handled the checks itself, the bank could have the $15 million in daily check receipts credited to its account at least one day sooner than through the Fed in St. Louis.

> In dollars, what did this acceleration of funds receipt by one day mean to First National? At the then 12% prime rate (the rate charged to favored customers), $15 million for one day was worth $5,000—for one day's worth of checks cleared one day earlier. If done every day, the savings to First National would be $25,000 per week or $1,300,000 per year!

> How did the First National Bank accomplish this neat trick? Every weekday morning the bank packed the

$15 million in checks into a large suitcase, which a messenger took aboard a Chicago-bound plane. Messenger, plane, and local fares cost, perhaps, $200 —for a saving of $5,000. Not bad.

Since 1974, two changes have occurred: The prime rate has dropped and inexorable inflation probably has increased the $15 million in daily check receipts to $20 million or more. So today, a one-day reduction in float probably saves the bank at least $4,000 per day.

Individuals cannot earn thousands a day by making their received checks clear into their accounts a day earlier, but as we shall see, they can enlarge their estates by many thousands through a thorough understanding of float—and how it can inure to their financial benefit.

Although the bank may have been limited to cutting float by one day, large businesses have found that they can cut float on incoming checks by several days.

Item: An Atlanta, Ga., insurance company found that, in addition to mail float and clearance float, it had to contend with "internal float" (also known as "incompetence float"). Its own clerks took an average of three days to process checks before they were deposited into the company account. This problem was simply and profitably solved by having checks sent to the company through a post office "lock box," and arranging for the company's bank to pick up the checks direct from the box, process them, and credit the company's account—all on the same day the checks were received, and at less than their previous internal cost.

This example is only the first step, yet it saved the insurance company three days of usually-lost float time.

The next step involves the transfer of money in Federal Funds. If a business (or an individual) has accounts in two banks, funds can be transferred almost instantaneously between the two accounts—provided a procedure is agreed upon in advance. Thus, by phone or wire, bank A is instructed to "wire" funds to bank B. The account in bank A is debited and the account in bank B is credited, in a simultaneous transaction. Likewise, bank A's Federal Reserve account is debited while bank B's account is credited.

A dozen or so years ago we could rest assured that a letter posted one day would arrive at its destination the next day if air mail were used for long distances. Today, with a 15¢ stamp, we feel fortunate if mail arrives in three or four days, denials by the Postal Service notwithstanding.

A New York based firm found that it took an average of four days for its pre-addressed envelopes to arrive from the West Coast. In addition, it took an average of *another* four days for the West Coast checks to clear into their account (clearance float). Hundreds of millions of dollars traveled from their western customers to the New York firm.

Their problem was solved, cutting total float from eight days to an average of 2.2 days. The company set up a "lock box" in Los Angeles and directed its customers to send remittances to the box instead of to New York. A bank in L.A. picked up the checks (several times a day), credited the firm's account, then wired Federal Funds daily as their checks cleared—which was one to two days later, since the overwhelming majority of checks received were drawn on West Coast banks. The cost of the service was minuscule compared to the savings realized by reduction of wasted float from 8 to 2.2 days—a net reduction of 5.8 days on several hundred million dollars:

$$\$100 \text{ million} \times 5.8 \text{ days @9\% per annum} =$$
$$(\text{approx.}) \ \$150,000.$$

It may be hard to believe that the individual can significantly increase the size of his or her nest-egg through the judicious use of float—but it *is* possible, as the reader will see as the full story unfolds.

> Item: At a Midwestern metals firm, one month's receipts totaled $65 million from 2,500 checks. Already operating four "lock boxes," the company, after careful analysis, added two more, rerouted receipts to the nearest box, and thereby reduced mail float to an average of 1.2 days for a further saving of 1.8 days on $65 million each month. The overall result was that this 1.8 day reduction of float improved the company's cash position by $2½ million, which was quickly used to reduce its short-term debt.

Recall that losses from float could be reduced in two ways: accelerating receipts and delaying payment. Thus far, examples of accelerating receipt of cash were given. Payment can also be slowed.

Everyone knows that it takes longer for a check to clear from an out-of-town bank than it does from a local one. Making use of this knowledge, many businesses open accounts at one or more distant or almost inaccessible banks, on which they draw checks to pay their bills. (Federal funds are transferred to these banks from their home accounts without any delay.) Through this device, they stretch out mail and clearance float by as much as an additional week, thus keeping the money in their accounts that much longer. This, of course, means that they can reduce their balance by a sum equal to a week's disbursements, resulting in a corresponding reduction in the amount of funds which need to be borrowed.

The business that is paid by a local customer with a check drawn on a bank three thousand miles away is not necessarily adversely affected by any increased clearance float, because Federal Reserve credits the bank's account within two days, and the bank will usually do the same for its good commercial customers.

> Item: Many companies pay their bills with checks drawn on particularly inaccessible banks (such as the First National Bank of West Plains, Mo.).

> Item: For bills payment, checks drawn on any bank in Tucson, Arizona, is a favorite, partieularly with East Coast firms. Why? There's no Federal Reserve Bank or branch in the entire state of Arizona. So checks must first clear through El Paso, Texas, which can add as much as two days to clearance float—in addition to the time required to clear checks from Texas to other distant states.

> Item: A large food company improved its cash position by $7 million through the simple expedient of having each regional division pay its bills with checks drawn on distant banks. The best arrangement was found to be having its entire West Coast division write checks on a bank in Richmond, Virginia, from where clearance time was found to be unusually long.

It has been shown how banks and businesses save or make large sums through an awareness that float presents opportunities for profit. The individual can do even more, but for a thorough understanding it is necessary to start with the most elementary method for turning float to your advantage. However, even the simple examples require a basic knowledge of interest-paying practices and how such interest is computed.

2.

In Your Best Interest

When money is borrowed from a bank, the borrower pays interest for every day that the loaned funds are in his possession. Until about ten years ago, however, when banks borrowed money from *individuals*, the individual was paid interest only if he left the money with the bank until the end of a quarterly or semi-annual period. (Remember, a deposit into a savings account is a loan of money to a bank at interest.) This is still the case with what is called "regular" savings accounts. Some of these accounts only earn interest on funds that are held by the bank for the entire quarter—from start to finish.

Although the "grace days" that are often offered in conjunction with "regular" accounts can be valuable, and will be discussed later, at this point we are concerned with a newer type of account, the one which pays interest from day of deposit to day of withdrawal (referred to in this book as DD-DW a/c). In such an account, interest is earned on money if it is in the account for only one day.

Simple interest, for the moment ignoring compounding, is computed in accordance with the formula:

$$I = P \times R \times T, \text{ where}$$

I = Interest earned
P = Principal (or amount of money on deposit)

R = Rate of Interest (per annum) expressed as a
        decimal (e.g., 5¼% = .0525)

T = Time (in years) that the principal is on
        deposit earning interest

Thus, for \$10,000 on deposit for one year at 5¼% (.0525) interest:

$$P = \$10,000$$
$$R = .0525$$
$$T = 1$$
$$I = P \times R \times T = \$10,000 \times .0525 \times 1$$

$$I = \$525.00$$

Actually, if interest is compounded *quarterly* (four times per year), \$10,000 @5¼% for one year earns \$535 in interest. If interest is compounded *continuously* (which, due to computers, means many times per *day*), interest is @5.47%. Nevertheless, at the moment, compounding of interest is inconsequential to us.

Since interest is earned daily in a DD-DW a/c, interest for one day is calculated by dividing the time (one year) by 365 days, or 1/365. Thus, interest for one day is:

$$I = \$10,000 \times .0525 \times 1/365 = \$1.44$$

Interest for three days is:

$$I = \$10,000 \times .0525 \times 1/365 \times 3 = \$4.32$$

Interest for seven days is:

$$I = \$10,000 \times .0525 \times 1/365 \times 7 = \$10.07$$

Note that at 5%, \$10,000 in one year grows to \$10,500, while at 5¼%, the sum becomes \$10,525. However, when we are dealing with but a few days interest, the difference between interest at 5% and 5¼% on $10,000 is minimal.

INTEREST	@ 5%	@ 5¼%
1 day	$1.37	$ 1.44
3 days	4.11	4.32
7 days	9.59	10.07

Mathematically, 5¼% yields 5% *more interest* than does 5%. Thus:

$$\$1.37 \text{ plus } (5\% \text{ of } \$1.37) = \$1.44$$

However, very often *much more* interest can be earned from a 5% account than one at 5¼%.

Since most people now have electronic calculators, and those who haven't can get them for as little as $5, daily interest calculation should be simple. However, for those who like to make mental calculations, daily interest can be *approximated* in the following manner:

1. Take the sum on which you wish to approximate one day's interest at 5% or 5¼%, for example, $10,000.

2. Move the decimal point to the left four places: $10,000. becomes $1.0,000 = $1.00

3. Add (approximately) 40% to that figure: $1.00 + .40 = $1.40

To approximate three days' interest on $10,000: $10,000 becomes $1.0,000 or $1.00 (as in 2. above)

Multiply by 3 (days) = $3.00

Add 40% of $3.00: $3.00 + $1.20 = $4.20

Now that computation of daily interest has been reviewed, let us move on to your checking account. Recall that Federal Reserve credits your bank with your deposit within two days after it is received by the Fed. But your bank does not clear the deposit *into* your account; it probably requires a longer clearance time before you can draw against check deposits, and for good reason:

If a business deposits a $5,000 check on Monday, uses the money on Wednesday, and the following Monday that $5,000 check is returned to the bank marked "Insufficient Funds," the odds are that the bank will not be stuck for the money—they are dealing with a going business. However, the *individual,* after using the $5,000 on Wednesday, *might disappear,* knowing in advance that the deposited check would "bounce." Were banks to allow automatic withdrawals against checks deposited two days previously, they would become sitting ducks for every con artist in the country.

So, unless cash is deposited, it is wise to be certain that before checks are written, checks to cover are deposited several days before—or else your check may bounce for "Uncleared Funds," with the attendant embarrassment and cost of $2 to $5 per bounced check.

The following chart, prepared by a major New York Commercial bank for the guidance of its own personnel, is based on the average number of business days, *excluding the day of deposit,* required for return of unpaid items (bounced checks). Employees of the bank are warned that "since experience varies and an item (check) could be properly returned at a later time than that indicated on the chart, no depositor should be advised of final payment of a check unless such payment has been verified with an officer of the drawee bank."

CITIES with delays differing from State	Under $2,500	$2,500 & Over	CITIES with delays differing from State	Under $2,500	$2,500 & Over
Atlanta	7	3	Los Angeles	8	5
Baltimore	6	3	Louisville	7	3
Birmingham	7	4	Memphis	7	4
Boston	6	3	Minneapolis	8	3
Buffalo	7	3	Nashville	7	4
Charlotte	7	4	New Orleans	7	3
Chicago	7	4	Oklahoma City	8	4
Cincinnati	7	3	Omaha	8	4
Cleveland	7	3	Philadelphia	6	3
Dallas	7	3	Pittsburgh	7	4
Denver	7	4	Portland, Ore.	8	5
Detroit	6	3	Richmond	7	4
El Paso	7	4	Salt Lake City	7	4
Helena	9	4	San Antonio	7	4
Houston	7	4	San Francisco	8	5
Jacksonville	7	4	Seattle	8	5
Kansas City, Ks.	8	4	St. Louis	7	4
Kansas City, Mo.	8	4	St. Paul	9	3
Little Rock	7	4			

STATES	Under $2,500	$2,500 & Over	STATES	Under $2,500	$2,500 & Over
Alabama	8	5	Nebraska	9	5
Arizona	9	5	Nevada	10	6
Arkansas	8	5	New Hampshire	7	5
California	9	6	New Jersey	6	4
Colorado	9	5	New Mexico	9	6
Connecticut	7	4	New York	6	4
Delaware	7	4	North Carolina	8	5
Dist. of Columbia	6	3	North Dakota	8	5
Florida	9	5	Ohio	8	5
Georgia	9	4	Oklahoma	8	5
Idaho	9	6	Oregon	9	6
Illinois	8	5	Pennsylvania	7	4
Indiana	8	5	Rhode Island	7	5
Iowa	8	5	South Carolina	9	4
Kansas	8	5	South Dakota	9	5
Kentucky	8	4	Tennessee	8	5
Louisiana	8	5	Texas	9	5
Maine	7	5	Utah	9	6
Maryland	8	4	Vermont	7	5
Massachusetts	7	5	Virginia	8	5
Michigan	7	4	Washington	10	6
Minnesota	9	4	West Virginia	8	4
Mississippi	8	5	Wisconsin	9	4
Missouri	9	4	Wyoming	9	6
Montana	10	6			

(continued on next page)

Figure 1. Transit Delay Chart (for checks deposited in N.Y.C.)

Transit Delay Chart (continued from previous page)

OUTSIDE CONTINENTAL U.S.	Under $2,500	$2,500 & Over
Alaska	10	7
Guam	11	9
Hawaii	10	9
Puerto Rico	10	6
Virgin Islands	10	6

Savings banks and savings and loan associations usually require longer periods of time for clearing check deposits, since
they must first deposit the checks into their commercial bank
and wait for any "bounced" items to be returned there before
the savings institution would receive it. This process adds a
minimum of two days to transit delay. Excluding the day of
deposit, savings institutions generally require from five to 20
business days before an individual can draw against a deposited
check drawn on a local or suburban bank. Longer periods may
be required for checks drawn on out-of-state banks.

Let us examine what the effects are of this delay in check
deposit clearance. First, your bank is credited with your deposit
sometime between your date of deposit and two days later, the
average time being just over one day. Meanwhile, you cannot
withdraw against that check for a *minimum* of five days (four
days plus the day of deposit). Thus, a deposit on Monday may
be used on Friday at the earliest, while deposits on later days
add *two to three* non-business days of the weekend. Therefore,
on average, you must wait a minimum of seven days—a calendar week—for the use of your money. Meanwhile, your bank
uses your money to earn interest. This is not quite as unfair as it
may sound, because today it costs banks about 30 cents to process each check, and many supply the service free, while others
charge a nominal fee of less than their cost. However, as reasonable as it may be, the net result is that you lose the use of your
deposits for one to two weeks due to clearance float.

This is not, nor is it meant to be a complete textbook on
banking; its purpose is to help the reader build an estate. Some
rudiments are included in the Historical Appendix so that the

devices for earning more money that are explained herein would be understood, and so that the reader would recognize new opportunities for increased earnings in coming years. So now, let us get to the first simple device, one that should repay you the cost of this book many times over—and continue to reward you year after year.

Start by taking your checkbook and adding up all the check deposits you made during the last 12 months. Your total may be more or less, but we will use the sum of $15,000 for the example.

Next, find out if your bank also issues day of deposit to day of withdrawal savings accounts (DD-DW a/c) paying 5% or 5¼% interest. While you are at it, check at your bank and at several other banks to learn their clearance time for deposited checks—local and out-of-town—for both check accounts and savings. In general, as has been previously noted, commercial banks will require less clearance time than savings banks. In addition, clearance time for savings accounts may be several days more than for check accounts at the same bank.

> Item: In the New York City area, just about all savings banks that offer free checking pay 5¼% on savings. Many commercial banks (e.g., Chase Manhattan) pay 5%, while some (e.g., Citibank) have paid only 4½%. Don't assume that your bank is paying 5% or 5¼%—ASK. Banks don't publicize it when they lower their interest rates.

For this (and several other) money-making devices, it is necessary to have *both* a DD-DW a/c and a checking a/c *at the same bank*. It is best if your "free" checking account has no minimum balance requirements. However, one that requires an *average monthly balance* of about $200 in *either* the checking a/c *or* the DD-DW savings a/c is O.K., because your balance will be in the latter account where it earns interest.

If your old checking a/c is at a bank that doesn't offer DD-

DW accounts paying at least 5%, switch banks to one that does. Whether at a new bank or your old one, open your new DD-DW a/c with approximately $300 in cash (or transfer of cleared funds from your checking a/c); deposit more if you have it available.

If your annual check deposits to your check account have averaged $15,000, your average weekly deposit has been about $300. As bills were paid or cash needed, most or all of the $300 was withdrawn by checks.

From now on, *do not* deposit any checks into your checking account. Deposit every check you receive into your DD-DW a/c. Whenever money is needed in your checking a/c, transfer funds from your DD-DW a/c to your checking a/c as described below.

> For example, if you have been depositing checks for $300 each week into your checking a/c, instead, deposit those checks into your DD-DW a/c and *at the same time* transfer $300 (or less if possible) into your checking a/c. You will see that no clearance time is required—checks can be drawn against transfer deposits immediately if the following described method is used.

> What will be accomplished? Previously, your deposited checks sat in a checking account for about a week waiting to be cleared. Under this new procedure, those checks will sit in a savings account where they will earn daily interest while waiting for clearance. Put another way, before this, when your checks went directly into your checking account, you would have been keeping a cleared balance to cover checks you wrote before your most recent deposit had cleared. That cleared balance of, say, $300 to $500 earned no interest, *and every dollar you have should work for you until it is spent* (and even longer, as you will learn).

Deposits into your DD-DW a/c are as simple as those to a checking account. You simply fill out a Savings Deposit slip. (See Fig. 2, pg. 26.) If you make a carbon copy of the deposit slip and describe each deposited item on the reverse side of the carbon copy, you will have a record of every check you received.

To transfer funds to your checking a/c at the same time, give the teller a Savings Withdrawal slip and a checking a/c Deposit slip. (See Figs. 3-A and 3-B, pgs. 27 and 28.)

Note that the deposit of $300 into the checking a/c is listed as *cash*. Your DD-DW passbook will show a deposit of $314.41 and a withdrawal of $300.

Assuming that your DD-DW a/c has a cleared balance of more than $300, the previous procedure can be simplified as shown in Figures 4-A and 4-B (pgs. 29 and 30). However, if the simplified method is used, your passbook will not show a deposit of $314.41 and withdrawal of $300, but only the net deposit of $14.41.

Passbook Savings Deposit

Deposited in The _____ Bank, and accepted subject to the provisions of the Uniform Commercial Code

We have an *Interest-In-Advance Savings Plan.* Ask your *Savings Advisor for details.*

Account Title (Print name as shown in passbook)

John Alert

Date	Savings Account Number	Trans
10	16	78	8 0 0 1 2 3 4 5	05

Shaded area for use only	Chk Cash'd
	Less Dep.
	Cash Ret'd

SAV 2 REV 3-78

Total $ Amt of Checks (in hundreds)		
		Begin Here
1 No Book		3 New Acct.

Passbook Savings Deposit

Cash	Dollars	Cents
Checks (List separately)		
1	287	40
2	25	37
3	1	64
4		
5		
6		
Total Deposit	314	41
Passbook or Computer Balance		

Figure 2. Sample Savings Deposit Slip

Passbook Savings Withdrawal

Take a loan instead of using your savings.
has Three Easy Ways to Borrow.

Date	Savings Account Number	Trans	Amount	Dollars	Cents
10 16 78	8 0 0 1 2 3 4 5	10	300	300	00

Amount (In Words) Three hundred $\frac{00}{xx}$ Dollars

Signature John Alert

Please is⁻ge Money Order(s) in the following amounts   Shaded area for ___ use only

If over $1,000, print Payee's Name

Dollars	Cents		MO/OC Number	Passbook or Computer Balance
300	00	Transfer to 800-1-098076		
		▼ Cash		1 No Book
300	00	▼ Total (Must be same as withdrawal amount)		

SAV 6 REV 4-78

Figure 3-A. Sample Savings Withdrawal Slip

Passbook Savings Withdrawal

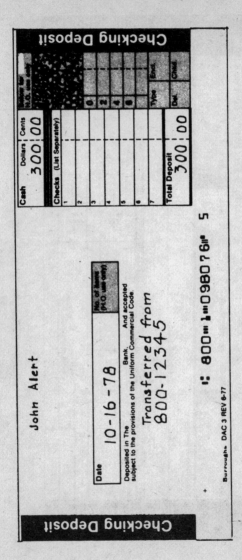

Figure 3-B: Sample Check Deposit Slip

Passbook Savings Deposit

Cash	Dollars	Cents
	1 4	4 1

Checks (List separately)

1	
2	
3	
4	
5	
6	

Total Deposit	1 4 4 1

Passbook or Computer Balance

Deposited in **The** **Bank,** and accepted subject to the provisions of the Uniform Commercial Code

We have an Interest-In-Advance Savings Plan. Ask your Savings Advisor for details.

Account Title (Print name as shown in passbook)

John Alert

Date		Savings Account Number		Trans
10 16 78		80 0 1 2 3 4 5		05

Shaded area for use only	Chk Cash'd	3 1 4 4 1	Total $ Amt of Checks (in hundreds)	← Begin Here
	Less Dep.	1 4 4 1		
	Cash Rec'd	300 00	1 No Book	3 New Acct.

SAV 2 REV 3-78

Passbook Savings Deposit

Figure 4-A. Simplified Savings Deposit Slip

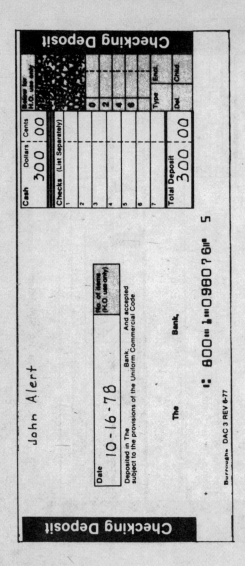

Figure 4-B. Check Deposit Slip for Simplified Transfer as a Cash Deposit

Learn to transfer money from your savings account only if it is needed to cover checks you write, so that your regular spendable funds earn daily interest—even if that interest is at the meager rate of 5% or 5¼%.

Assuming an average total annual deposit of checks to be $15,000, the simple device described above earns an extra (approx.) $15. Fifteen dollars is not an impressive sum, but it is only the beginning. When used in conjunction with other methods of money management described later, this elementary procedure can result in an addition of $2,000 to the nest-egg of Mr. or Ms. Average Reader. So as skiers think snow, think $2,000, not $15. By the time you've read the last page you will understand how simple it is to build that large estate.

Some people may balk at the necessity of going to a bank at specific times during the month in order to pick up a few dollars in extra interest. And many of us may say that our time is worth more—more than the few dollars gain from the stop at the bank.

By the same rationale, it wouldn't be worth our time to shop for bargains at the supermarket, comb the newspapers for "cents off" coupons, mow the lawns and shovel the snow from our walks. But money-wise, inflation-ravaged consumers do all these things because they know that time is only *worth* more if they can *earn* more during those hours they spend with the grass or snow.

Spare time spent scouting for money bargains becomes an interesting adventure, a game of beating the system—the banking system. A highly profitable game.

3.

The Answer:
What It Isn't,
What It Is . . . .

The previously described simple method for earning extra dollars is based upon a way to earn interest on checks received while waiting for those checks to clear into a checking account. This device may interest some people, but in one part of the country, the New England States, people have found a better way.

For some years now, residents of Maine, New Hampshire, Vermont, Massachusetts, Connecticut, and Rhode Island have enjoyed the benefits of what are called NOW accounts. NOW stands for Negotiable Order of Withdrawal, an important feature of a type of account available in those states from commercial banks, savings banks, and savings and loan associations. It is, basically, a savings account on which "negotiable orders of withdrawal" (checks) can be written. Since it is a savings account, the balances earn interest.

People who have the accounts love them. Even the American Bankers Association (but not the smaller Independent Bankers Association of America) supported legislation which made NOW accounts available nationally. This legislation *may be* in the public interest, but for those (like the readers of this book) who are looking to increase the return on their savings, nationally available NOW accounts may be a double-edged sword. An explanation is in order.

Historically, the Federal Reserve has prohibited member banks from paying interest on demand (checking) accounts. Savings banks that offer checking accounts, and which are not members of the Federal Reserve System, have likewise been so prohibited by state laws or regulations of their insuring agency.

However, many banks in Massachusetts insure deposits through a state insurance fund rather than through the F.D.I.C. and are not member banks of the Fed. Therefore, these banks are not subject to the regulations or prohibitions of the federal agencies, and must conform only to their state's requirements.

After successful litigation in the Massachusetts courts, the Consumers Savings Bank in Worcester, Mass., came out with the NOW account, the savings account on which the equivalent of checks could be drawn—in reality, a checking account that paid interest.

In Massachusetts, the many banks under federal control, such as commercial banks which are members of Federal Reserve, could not compete with the NOW accounts. To summarize the ensuing lengthy battle, after two special Acts of the U.S. Congress, all three major types of banking institutions in all of the six New England states can, and do, offer the NOW account. And there were strong pressures to make the account available all over the nation by removing the prohibition against paying interest on demand deposits.

On the surface, it sounds good for everybody except the banks—which would finally have to pay interest on the monies that sit in check account balances, funds that the banks use to make profitable loans.

But it's a mirage.

Although check account balances are a big source of income for banks, checking accounts are a costly expense, to the tune of about 30¢ for each check written. Twenty-five billion checks at

30¢ each comes to the tidy sum of $7½ billion—and banks cover a good part of that cost from their earnings on checking account balances. That's why we get check accounts for free, or for 10¢ to 15¢ a check.

If banks lose a good part of their check-balance income by having to pay interest on those balances, their loss of income will be made up somewhere else. There are many "somewhere elses."

Until now, Fed. member banks received no interest on reserve balances on deposit at the Fed. One definite probability is that the Federal Reserve Banks will start paying member banks interest on reserve balances. This will decrease the Fed.'s income—of which 90% has been paid annually to the U.S. Treasury. That billion dollars a year that the Treasury would lose will be made up to the Treasury—as made up it must be—by a corresponding increase in our income taxes. Or, of course, the Fed. can pay the interest to the banks and still maintain its own profits by charging the banks a higher discount rate for advances. But that increased cost to the banks will be passed on; interest rates on loans to business and individuals will go up. Interest rates are one of the costs of doing business. If those rates go up, prices go up. It will be either higher taxes or higher prices —or both. Either way, you lose.

Secondly, free checking accounts could become an amenity of the past. We'll pay 30¢ or more for every check we write—and possibly some fee for every check we deposit. If banks have to pay interest on checking balances, thereby losing a major source of income, you can bet that the banks will make it up—in spades. And perhaps that is why the American Bankers Association favored national legalization of the NOW accounts or their equivalent.

And why is it in the best interest of our readers that NOW accounts *not* go national? Let's see who pays for this kind of "do-good" legislation.

Federally mandated low interest rates on savings accounts subsidize the private home mortgage market. Mortgage loans are a "Best Buy." Why? Because someone other than the mortgage giver or taker is forced to pay some of its cost. That someone is YOU.

Next, an analogy:

When the United Auto Workers strikes General Motors for higher wages and wins, the workers think they have it made. They will get more for the same work. But that, too, is a mirage.

G.M. raises its prices to compensate for its increased costs. With higher prices for cars, trucks and busses, the cost of all transportation goes up, raising the cost of everything that moves —food, clothing, material goods. The steel or bakery or farm worker pays higher prices because of the G.M. raise, so he, too, "needs" higher wages. More raises, more price increases.

And before that U.A.W. member has a chance to enjoy his increased wages, he finds that higher prices have left him where he was before his raise—or worse.

The lesson: The U.A.W. member would benefit from his pay increase only if his employer did not (or could not) pass the cost on to the general public—or if the U.A.W. member got his raise, but other workers didn't (or couldn't).

Starting November 1, 1978, new federal regulations permitted banks all over the country to offer *almost* the equivalent of NOW accounts. As of that date, combination savings and checking accounts have been available wherein funds are *automatically* transferred from savings to checking whenever needed to cover checks.

Having received an announcement from a local savings bank (see Fig. 5, pg. 37), a check at several savings and commercial banks revealed that this attractive service will not be free.

Anticipated charges vary from $2.50 per month ($30 per year) to 25¢ or 50¢ per transaction. Additionally or alternately, a minimum balance of $500 will be required in the savings accounts (in excess of amounts to be automatically transferred to cover checks). This latter requirement means that more than $500 must be tied up indefinitely at the bank's *lowest* interest rate (5% or 5¼%) instead of the highest rate (7¾% or 8%).

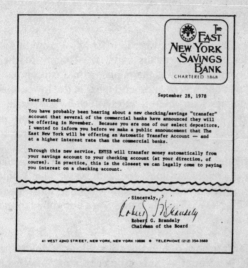

The East
New York
Savings
Bank
CHARTERED 1868

September 28, 1978

Dear Friend:

You have probably been hearing about a new checking/savings "transfer" account that several of the commercial banks have announced they will be offering in November. Because you are one of our select depositors, I wanted to inform you before we make a public announcement that The East New York will be offering an Automatic Transfer Account — and at a higher interest rate than the commercial banks.

Through this new service, ENYSB will transfer money automatically from your savings account to your checking account (at your direction, of course). In practice, this is the closest we can legally come to paying you interest on a checking account.

Sincerely,

Robert G. Brandely
Chairman of the Board

41 WEST 42ND STREET, NEW YORK, NEW YORK 10036 • TELEPHONE (212) 354-3560

Fig. 5. Announcement from local savings bank.

$500 for one year, compounded continuously, yields: $27.35 at 5¼% and $42.25 at 8%—a difference of $14.90 in one year. And if you keep the account for eight years, the difference, because of compounding, becomes $191.17 (interest on $500 for eight years equals $456.77 at 8%, $265.60 at 5¼%). In 20 years, your interest loss reaches $1,081.96!—quite a cost for the convenience of automatically transferring funds from savings to checking. And the cost will actually be higher, since the balance in savings must be *more than* $500 to allow for transfers to checking when needed.

Unless Automatic Transfer Accounts are really free and without minimum balance requirements, avoid them and do your own transferring of funds as previously and later described. You can make even more than you will save.

Many banks did not follow through with Automatic Transfer Accounts because, as of January 1, 1979, the rules were finally changed to permit banks other than those in New England to issue NOW accounts.

If the banking industry were to offer NOW accounts with the same rules and requirements as those of many of their New England compatriots, we, the public, would end up paying for the service in one way or another (higher taxes, lower interest on savings, higher loan interest rates which would result in still higher prices). But it hasn't happened. The New York bankers found a better way—to insure their continued incomes.

The original New England NOW accounts offered interest on checking balances without (or with very small) minimum balance requirements. The result was that most banks lost money with NOW. The big banks were not about to make the same mistakes.

With fanfare born of hundreds of millions of dollars in advertising, NOW accounts—"interest on checking"—were heralded far and wide. In *small* print were the minimum balance requirements—requirements which insure good income to the banks at the NOW account holders' expense.

All of the new NOWs require either a *minimum* monthly balance or a *minimum average* daily balance in order to avoid charges of as much as $5 per month. Figure 6 (page 39) explains Chase Manhattan's $3,000 *minimum* monthly balance and charges incurred should the balance fall below that minimum. Note that both the NOW account and the Chase regular savings account pay 5% interest.

The Chase Manhattan Bank, N.A.
1 Chase Manhattan Plaza
New York, New York 10015

Richard P. O'Neill
Vice President

CHASE

Dear Chase Checking Customer:

You have probably been hearing a lot about getting interest on checking, and frankly, all that talk can get very confusing.

That's why we at Chase are sending you this letter. We want to clear away any possible confusion by answering questions which you are likely to have about this new way to earn interest. Hopefully, these answers will help you decide whether Interest on Checking at Chase is right for you.

How does Interest on Checking at Chase work?

It's very simple. It works just like any checking account—except it pays interest. At Chase, Interest on Checking is available with all personal and fiduciary accounts.

What rate of interest will Chase pay?

Chase will pay the highest rate you can get anywhere—5%. No other bank, including savings banks can pay a higher rate on this type of account. In addition, Chase will compound the interest daily to increase your interest yield to 5.20%—again the highest you can get, and other banks might not offer a yield this high.

How often will Chase pay the interest to my account?

You will receive your interest on the first business day of each month.

How much does this service cost?

At Chase, it is absolutely free if you maintain a minimum monthly balance of $3,000 or more in either this checking account, or a Chase regular savings account or divided between these two accounts. There are never any per check charges. If, however, your combined minimum monthly balance falls between $2,000 and $2,999, there is a monthly service charge of only $2.50; below $2,000, the charge is $5.00.

But, it may be worthwhile for you to get this service free . . . even if it means moving money you keep in other banks to Chase. Remember, no other bank including savings banks can pay you a higher rate on this type of account. So even if your money is earning 5¼% at a savings bank, and you move it to Chase, you give up only ¼ of 1%. On $3,000, this amounts to about $11.40 per year. The interest you earn on your checking balance will probably more than make up this difference.

How do I get Interest on Checking at Chase?

You can open your account right now and begin earning interest on your checking balances. Just stop by your Chase branch, and we'll open an account for you in a matter of minutes.

Very truly yours,

Richard P. O'Neill

Richard P. O'Neill

Fig. 6. Chase Manhattan's NOW Accounts described.

There is a big difference between *minimum* and *minimum average* balance requirements. With a *minimum* balance requirement of $3,000, should the balance fall below that figure —even by 1¢ for one day—the service charge will be assessed, even if the balance has greatly exceeded the minimum for 29 of the 30 days in the month. Marine Midland describes their *minimum average* requirement thusly: ". . . it's free if you keep $1,000 average daily balance in your account. So if you drop below that amount during the month, then later make a large deposit—as long as you maintain the average, there's no charge."

Chemical Bank is one of the very few offering an option. Maintain *either* a *minimum* balance of $2,000 *or* a *minimum average* daily balance of $3,000 to avoid a monthly service charge.

It should be realized that if you are required to maintain a minimum balance (of $2,000 for example), your average balance will be much higher—unless you make a deposit each time you write a check. Chemical Bank's requirements are realistic—an *average* balance will generally exceed a *minimum* balance by some sum close to $1,000. Therefore, if you intend to open a NOW account with a minimum-balance requirement, it would be best to assume that you will keep an average of $500 to $1,000 in excess of the minimum requirement tied up in the bank earning only 5% interest.

Following is a table showing the variations of balance requirements and service charges for NOW accounts among several typical banking institutions.

	Minimum Balance	Minimum Average Balance	Monthly Service Charge If Below Minimum	Probable Average Balance To Avoid Service Charges
Chase Manhattan	$3,000	---	$2.50 - $5	$4,000
Chemical Bank	2,000	$3,000	$4	3,200
Marine-Midland	---	1,000	$4	1,300
Anchor Savings	1,000	---	$2	1,600
Williamsburgh Savings	---	1,000	$2 - $3	1,300
Metropolitan Savings	1,000	---	$2	1,600
West Side Fed. S&L	500	---	$2	1,100

Let us see what NOW checking can cost *you*—as compared to a really free checking account (see Fig. 7, below), used in conjunction with a day-of-deposit to day-of-withdrawal (DD-DW) savings account, as described in a previous chapter.

Fig. 7. Free Checking (not a NOW Account).

Depending upon the requirements of the banks in your neighborhood, you will probably keep an average balance of $1,100 to $4,000 in a NOW account (see chart). A checking account is usually kept for many, many years. That means that you will keep $1,100 to $4,000 tied up for many years earning 5% interest (yielding a maximum of 5.20%).

In eight years, at 5%, compounded to yield 5.20%,
$1,100 will earn $550.13 and
$4,000 will earn $2,000.48.

However, instead of keeping an average balance of $1,100 to $4,000 in a NOW account in order to earn 5% interest, suppose you kept your free checking account (as described in Figure 7, page 41), with no minimum balance requirements and deposited funds into the account only when needed to cover checks. Then you could put that $1,100 to $4,000 into an eight-year or more savings certificate paying 8%, compounded to yield 8.45%.

In eight years, at 8%, compounded to yield 8.45%,
$1,100 will earn $1,004.89 (compared to $550.13 at 5%) &
$4,000 will earn $3,654.14 (compared to $2,000.48 at 5%).

Therefore, to "earn interest on checking" with a NOW account, you've lost—over an eight-year period—between $454.76 on a $1,100 average balance ($1,004.89 − $550.13) and $1,653.66 on a $4,000 average balance ($3,654.14 − $2,000.48).

With NOW, the banks giveth (5%) and the banks taketh away (8%). With the income-increasing methods described in this book, the gains you make are yours to keep.

NOW may have been a good deal in New England, but is it for you?

Don't bank on it!

With income taxes, when a select few exploit a tax loophole, those few gain—and all the rest of us pay for it. It is the same with interest-increasing devices; if a select few use them, those few will gain. If everyone uses them, everyone *appears* to gain, but everyone will pay for it. The moral? If you want to profit from banking tricks, keep them to yourself.

The next few pages are devoted to ways by which interest can be increased. Although many of these methods have been used successfully for many years now, the banking industry in general has not stopped their use by changing their regulations.

If you are not acquainted with some of these "tricks," learn them, but don't rush to use them—yet. Later, you will see that they can be refined to yield much greater gains for you.

First, the difference between a "regular savings account" (Reg. a/c) and a "day of deposit to day of withdrawal savings account" (DD-DW a/c) should be understood. (See Fig. 8, below.)

The DD-DW a/c, as previously explained, earns interest on every dollar for every day that it is in the account. Even if a deposit is made one day and withdrawn the next day, the dollars withdrawn will have earned one day's interest.

The Reg. a/c pays interest from the day of deposit only *if the deposit remains in the account until the end of the quarter.* Therefore, for example, a deposit made on January 5th and withdrawn on March 20th will not earn one cent in interest. However, many banks, as an incentive, offer that deposits made by the 10th of any month will earn interest from the first of that month, provided the funds remain until the end of that quarter. (See Fig. 8, below.) These 10-day periods are called "grace days."

Day-to-Day Savings Accounts

5.47% is the effective annual yield on **5.25%** a year.* Dividends are paid for every day your funds are on deposit provided a balance of $25 remains on deposit to the end of the quarterly period.

Regular Savings Accounts

5.47% is the effective annual yield on **5.25%** a year.* Dividends are paid from day of deposit on all balances of $25 or more—deposits made on or before the tenth day of any month earn dividends from the first of that month.

*Latest Dividend

Interest and dividends on all accounts are compounded daily and credited quarterly. Savings earn the maximum effective annual rate when deposits remain in your account for a year and the accumulated interest/dividends are not withdrawn.

Fig. 8. Regular Savings Account vs. Day-of-Deposit to Day-of-Withdrawal Savings Account.

It is easy to see what many people do. During most of the year, they use only their DD-DW a/c. However, on the 10th of the third month of each quarter (March, June, September, and December), they withdraw a major part of their funds from the DD-DW a/c and deposit it into the Reg. a/c, leaving it there from the 10th to the end of the month (which is also the end of the quarter).

At the end of the quarter, leaving only a minimum balance in the Reg. a/c, the bulk of money is withdrawn from the Reg. a/c and deposited into the DD-DW a/c where it is available at any time without loss of interest.

From the 1st through the 10th, the same money earns interest in both accounts—that's 10% for 10 days, four times a year. If, for example, $10,000 was moved from one account to the other, the *additional* interest amounts to approximately $15 each quarter, or $60 a year.

If both accounts pay 5.25% (to yield 5.47%), this switching increases the annual rate to about 5.85% with a yield of over 6%.

One-year certificates pay 6.5% (to yield 6.81%), but funds are tied up for the full year. Switching funds between a DD-DW a/c and a Reg. a/c keeps the funds available at any time. (Savings certificates, which are time deposit accounts, will be discussed in a later chapter.)

Some savings and loan associations combine the benefits of the DD-DW a/c and the Reg. a/c, offering daily interest plus the 10 grace days each month. However, to accomplish the same result (temporary double interest), it is still necessary to use two accounts, withdrawing from one and depositing into the other on the 10th of the last month of the quarter.

Next, in addition to the 10 grace days, many banks permit withdrawals from regular accounts during the last three business days of each quarter without loss of interest. If the last day of the quarter (March 31, June 30, September 30, December 31) falls on Sunday through Tuesday, funds can be withdrawn five calendar days before the end of the month, since two non-business weekend days split the last three business days. If month's end falls on Wednesday through Friday, withdrawals can be made only three calendar days prior to month's end.

The three business days during which withdrawals can be made without interest loss are known as "bonus days" and average out to four calendar days during which interest is earned even if funds have been withdrawn.

It should be obvious that the bonus days can be added to the 10 grace days to give a total of 13 (or 14) days each quarter during which double interest can be earned. Thus, the additional interest on $10,000 amounts to $20 quarterly, or $80 annually. Put another way, combining grace and bonus days four times a year increases the nominal annual interest rate of 5.25% to 6%.

Example

On March 10, 1978, $10,000 is withdrawn from a DD-DW a/c and deposited into a Reg. a/c. On March 29th (the 3rd business day before the end of the quarter), $10,000 is withdrawn from the Reg. a/c and deposited into the DD-DW a/c.

1. During the first 10 days and the last three days of March, the $10,000 earned interest at the rate of 5.25% from each of the two accounts, to a total of 10.5%.

2. For the month of March, the $10,000 earned (approximately) $45 from the Reg. a/c plus almost $19 from the DD-DW a/c, to a total of $64.

3. For the month of March, the $10,000 earned in-

terest at the rate of 7.5%. This rate was accomplished
without having to tie up the principal for a year or
more in a certificate.

Good as these extra earnings on "liquid funds" may appear
to be, hold them in abeyance until you have finished reading.
Better returns are in the offing.

It is important that the reader understand each technique that
can be used to construct a game plan for saving money, making
money, and building an estate. That is why the *best* way to earn
the highest return on money is not described at this point.

The 3 P.M. Rule

Let's turn for a moment to the commercial banks.

In the good old days, bankers' hours were 9 A.M. to 3 P.M.
Not any more. Early morning and late evening hours are com-
monplace with all types of banking institutions. And even here
we find the opportunity to turn an extra dollar.

Old traditions die hard. The old-time bank day of 9 A.M. to 3
P.M. hangs on at commercial banks. Many display a sign (or
have printed in their rules): "Transactions made after 3 P.M.
are effective on the next business day." This, of course, means
that if money is deposited into a savings account on Friday
evening, it will not start to earn interest until the following Monday (or Tuesday if a bank holiday falls on Monday).

And it also means that money taken *out* of a savings account
continues to earn interest over the weekend (provided that the
account pays interest to day of withdrawal).

In contrast to the practice of commercial banks, savings
banks and savings and loan associations seldom, if ever, have
the 3 P.M. rule. And because of this difference in rules, it is
possible to earn double interest for three to four days each
week.

Example

(In both theory and practice this method works, but constant use would become a nuisance to the depositor.)

1. After 3 P.M. on Friday, withdraw $10,000 from the DD-DW a/c in the commercial bank. (The withdrawal is entered into the passbook as of the following Monday.)

2. The same afternoon or evening, deposit the $10,000 into the DD-DW a/c in the savings bank. (The deposit is entered into the passbook as of Friday.)

3. Result: $10,000 earns interest from Friday to Monday in both accounts—and that's three extra days of interest over the weekend. (If Monday is a bank holiday, four extra days of interest are earned.)

4. If the transaction was made by teller's check, the deposit into the savings bank would have to clear before the money could be returned to the commercial bank's account in order to repeat the process.

5. Again, don't rush to try this little trick; there are better ways to accomplish even more.

Just for a moment, let us refer back to the first simple device. Recall that deposits were put into the DD-DW a/c so that interest was earned on balances from the date of deposit until the funds were needed in the checking account.

If your savings and checking accounts are at a commercial bank (with the 3 P.M. rule), and if the deposit into the DD-DW a/c is made before 3 P.M., and the transfer of funds into the checking a/c is made after 3 P.M. (or if a cash withdrawal is made from the DD-DW a/c after 3 P.M.), an extra day of interest is picked up on weekdays and three days on Fridays. But unless the deposit and/or withdrawal is of great magnitude, it would hardly pay to bother. (One day's interest on $10,000 is $1.37, while it is only 14¢ on $1,000.)

But the 3 P.M. rule offers more. Together with grace and bonus days, alert depositors have found it worthwhile to have more than one checking account as well as several savings accounts.

Example

Mr. Alert has both a checking account and a DD-DW savings account at his neighborhood commercial bank. Transactions can be made daily from 8 A.M. to 4 P.M., and until 7 P.M. on Fridays. For easy reference we'll call these accounts CB/Check a/c and CB/DD-DW a/c.

Around the corner from the commercial bank is a savings bank which services its customers daily from 8:30 A.M. to 6:30 P.M. and until 8:00 P.M. on Fridays (and half days on Saturdays). At this bank Mr. Alert has a free checking account (SB/Check a/c) and two savings accounts (SB/DD-DW a/c and SB/Reg. a/c).

Recap

Commercial Bank	Savings Bank
1. CB/Check a/c	3. SB/Check a/c
2. CB/DD-DW a/c	4. SB/DD-DW a/c
	5. SB/Reg. a/c

Account #2 (CB/DD-DW a/c) has a balance of more than $10,000. The other four accounts (#1, #3, #4, and #5) have negligible or minimal balances. It is March 1978.

March 1978

Sun	Mon	Tue	Wed	Thu	Fri	Sat
			1	2	3	4
5	6	7	8	9	10	11
12	13	14	15	16	17	18
19	20	21	22	23	24	25
26	27	28	29	30	31	

On Friday evening, March 10th, Mr. Alert transfers $10,000 from his CB/DD-DW a/c (#2) to his CB/Check a/c (#1). Since it is after 3 P.M., the transfer is dated and entered as of Monday, March 13th. (See Figs. 9A & 9B, pgs. 50, 51.)

Next, he writes a check for $10,000 payable to himself and drawn on his CB/Check a/c (#1)—into which he has just transferred $10,000 from his CB/DD-DW a/c (#2). Mr. Alert endorses this check for deposit into his SB/Reg. a/c (#5) (which, if you will recall, gives "Interest from the first on deposits made through the 10th of any month"). At the savings bank around the corner, he deposits this check into his SB/Reg. a/c (#5). (See Figs. 10A & 10B, pgs. 52, 53.)

Take a loan instead of using your savings.
___ has Three Easy Ways to Borrow.

Passbook Savings Withdrawal

Date	Savings Account Number	Trans	Amount		
				Dollars	Cents
3 13 78	80 01 12345	10	10,000		00

Amount (In Words)

Ten Thousand 00/xx _____ Dollars

Signature   John B. Alert

Please issue Money Order(s) in the following amounts   If over $1,000, print Payee's Name

Dollars	Cents		MO/OC Number	Passbook or Computer Balance
10,000	00	Transfer to		
		800-1-098 076		
▼ Cash				
▼ Total (Must be same as withdrawal amount)			1 No Book	
10,000	00			

Shaded area for ___ use only

SAV 6 REV 4-78

9A: Passbook Savings Withdrawal.

Passbook Savings Withdrawal

Transferred from
800-12345

Save time! Use your personalized, pre-numbered checking deposit forms. If you need more, ask teller for reorder form.

Deposited in The
The Uniform Commercial Code.   Bank,   and accepted subject to the conditions of

Account Title (Name)

John B. Alert

Date	Checking Account Number
3-13-78	8 0 0 1 1 0 9 8 0 7 6

DAC 1A REV. 6-77

Checking Deposit

	Cash	Dollars	Cents		Below for H.O. Use Only Number of Items
		10,000	00		
Checks (List separately)					0
1					2
2					4
3					5
4					6
5					
6					
7				Type	Enc. Del. Chkd.
Total Deposit		10,000	00		

9B: Checking Deposit.

10A. Commercial Bank/Checking Account check.

10B: Savings Bank/Regular Account Passbook Deposit slip.

Thus, using the 3 P.M. rule and taking advantage of check float, accounts #2 (CB/DD-DW a/c) and #5 (SB/Reg. a/c) both earn interest for the first 13 days of March—at a total rate of 10¼%. And the $10,000 plus interest can be withdrawn from account #5 on March 29th and still earn interest through March 31st.

It should be realized that if the money is allowed to
remain in account #5 (SB/Reg. a/c) after March 31st,
interest will be earned only if the money remains in
the account through the end of June, since account #5
is a regular account and does not pay interest to day
of withdrawal. So, sometime between March 29th
and 31st, Mr. Alert transfers most of the balance in
account #5 to his account #4 (SB/DD-DW a/c) where
it earns interest from day of deposit to day of
withdrawal.

At this point it may be well to explain a fine point in the computation of daily interest—as figured for DD-DW accounts. If a
sum is deposited on, for example, March 14th and the same
amount withdrawn on the 24th, 10 days worth of daily interest
is earned (24 minus 14 equals 10). It is commonly believed that if
a deposit is made on the 1st of the month and withdrawn on the
31st, a full month's interest for 31 days will be earned. However, the deposit earns interest for only 30 days, not the full 31
(31 minus 1 equals 30).

Rule: In a day of deposit to day of withdrawal account (DD-DW a/c), the day that a deposit is made is
not a day on which the deposit earns interest. However, interest is earned for the day on which money is
withdrawn.

With a regular savings account (Reg. a/c) that offers
interest from the first day if deposited by the 10th, a
deposit made on any day from the 1st through the
10th will earn interest from and including the 1st.

The reader may realize that in the last example Mr. Alert did
not take advantage of the three bonus days at the end of the
quarter. He could have done the following:

(Mr. Alert's Example continued.)

On Tuesday, March 28th, Mr. Alert writes a check drawn on his SB/Check a/c (#3) for $10,000 to himself and endorses it for deposit to his CB/DD-DW a/c (#2). [Recall that he had withdrawn $10,000 from this account #2 on March 13th for transfer to his account #1 (CB/Check a/c) at the same commercial bank.] Now, he deposits this $10,000 check into his account #2. (See Figs. 11 and 12, pgs. 56, 57.)

The following day, March 29th, Mr. Alert transfers $10,000 from his SB/Reg. a/c (#5) to his SB/Check a/c (#3) to cover the check he issued the day before. Since the money is withdrawn from the regular savings account during the last three business days (bonus days), interest is earned in that account for the full 31 days in March. In addition, interest is earned in account #2 (CB/DD-DW a/c) from the 28th through the 31st, or three days.

In total, using check float, and grace and bonus days, double interest can be earned for the first 13 and last three days of the month.

However, it was noted on page 54 that Mr. Alert did *not* take advantage of the bonus days at the end of the quarter. He didn't for a practical reason: With no additional effort, he knew he could pick up an additional 11 days of double interest instead of the three offered by the bonus days. We'll come to this later.

Another Way To Beat the Bank—Cash Reserve

Some readers may have noticed that Mr. Alert wrote and used checks *before* he had deposited money to cover them. And some may recall the admonition: avoid issuing checks against uncollected funds and *never* issue checks against undeposited funds. In recent years, banks have offered a service that makes it altogether legal and proper to pass checks drawn against uncollected or undeposited funds—it is a tool with which one's

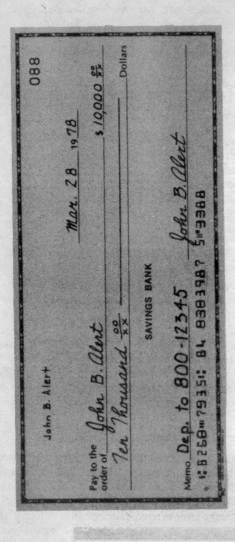

Fig. 11: Savings Bank check (for deposit to Savings Account in Commercial Bank).

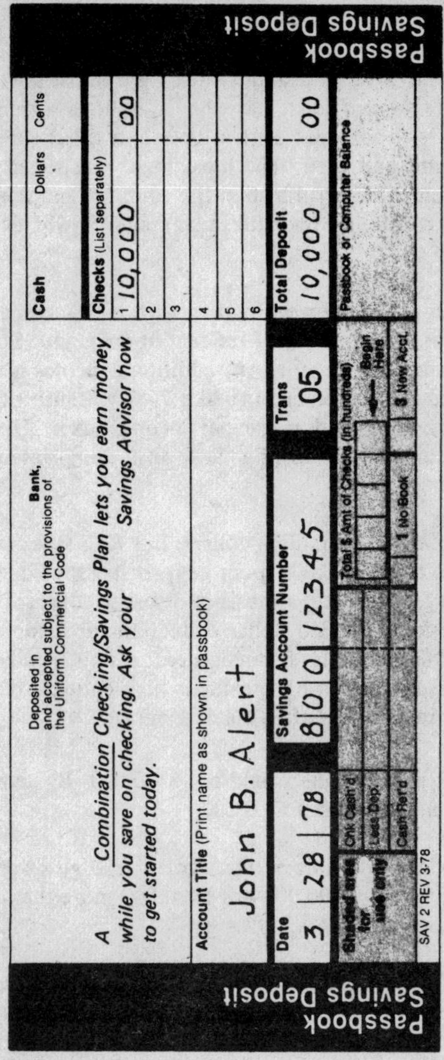

	Cash	Dollars	Cents
Checks (List separately)			
1		10,000	00
2			
3			
4			
5			
6			
Total Deposit		10,000	00
Passbook or Computer Balance			

Deposited in
and accepted subject to the provisions of
the Uniform Commercial Code

Bank,

*A ____ Combination Checking/Savings Plan lets you earn money
while you save on checking. Ask your ____ Savings Advisor how
to get started today.*

Account Title (Print name as shown in passbook)

John B. Alert

Date			Savings Account Number	Trans
3	28	78	8 0 0 1 2 3 4 5	05

Shaded area
for
Bank only:
Chk Cashd
Less Dep.
Cash Rec'd

Total $ Amt of Checks (in hundreds)

Begin Here

1 No Book   3 New Acct.

SAV 2 REV 3-78

Passbook Savings Deposit

Fig. 12: Commercial Bank Savings Account deposit slip.

financial management problems can be eased and it can even be used as the key to sizable earnings.

And let there be no mistake about one's right to use anything to one's advantage—provided that what is done is within the law and the rules. Loopholes exist in laws and rules; they are there to be found and used. The most highly respected, the wealthiest, the most powerful men in the country, and the biggest businesses constantly take full advantage of whatever is allowed by law.

Take the example of the wealthy man with high income. He could be, and has often been, the President of the United States, the Vice President, or a Senator. Any additional income he may earn will be reduced by something like 70% because of top bracket federal, state, and municipal income taxes. He has something of value that has cost him little or nothing—as an example, Presidential papers.

He could sell them for a million dollars. But 70% taxes would leave him with a mere $300,000 (poor guy). Instead, he donates them to a library, university, a museum or other non-profit institution, and takes a million dollar deduction for income tax purposes. This million dollar deduction reduces his income tax by $700,000 (assuming that his income is high enough to keep him in a 70% bracket even after the deduction).

By selling his property, he would net $300,000. By giving it away, the philanthropist nets $700,000.

Everybody wins. The library (etc.) got a free gift worth a million. The donor got $700,000—or $400,000 more than if he had sold his property.

But that $700,00 not paid in taxes must be made up by someone. Government won't spend less because they didn't collect the $700,000. The someone who makes up the deficit is you and me!

But it's all legal, ethical, and even moral!

Other examples of using a service (or loophole) to one's advantage is the profitable exploitation of "float," as described in Chapter I. If there is one lesson to learn from this it is that, if big companies and prominent people can take advantage of quirks in the banking system and tax laws, so can you. And don't imagine it is cheating—it's playing the game according to the rules set down by the banks, not by you.

Knowledge of check clearance time, applicable regulations, and special bank services can be the key to more profitable personal financial management.

One such special bank service now permits the writing of checks against uncollected and even undeposited funds—and the checks won't bounce. Even if one never expects to borrow money from a bank, this service is an invaluable adjunct to a checking account, gives the equivalent of *instantaneous* clearance for your deposits, and makes possible heretofore unheard of interest earnings.

This service is offered by commercial banks across the country and is called Cash Reserve, or any of dozens of other names. Basically, it sets up a credit line of $500 to $5,000 (and even as much as $15,000) tied directly to one's checking account so that funds are automatically advanced to one's account, up to the prearranged limit, to cover any overdraft, thus preventing such checks from bouncing. Of course, banks charge interest, usually at the rate of 12% per year, for advancing monies to the checking account customer.

But that isn't all that a Cash Reserve does. Its other features are valuable and *without cost!* We "have a friend at Chase Manhattan," John J. (Jack) Toolan, who patiently reviewed for us just how Cash Reserve works.

1. Assume your checking account balance is $200. You write

a check for $305 which, when it comes back to your bank is refused because of insufficient funds. You are charged a service charge (S/C) of $4, your balance is reduced to $196, and your $305 bill remains unpaid. That's *bad*. In some places you can even be charged with a crime!

2. Next, assume the same circumstances, except that you deposited by check $350 a day or two before your $305 check comes back to your bank. Your balance shows $550 ($200 + $350), yet when that $305 check comes back to your bank, it is also rejected, but this time because the check was drawn against uncollected funds. Again you pay a $4 service charge, but this time if the recipient of your $305 check redeposits it after its return to him, it will clear. That's not *so* bad, but *not good*.

3. Now, with the same situation as No. 1 above, but with Cash Reserve, your account would appear thus:

Date	Checks	Deposits	Balance	Cash Reserve In Use
1/31			$200	0
2/5	$305	(CR) $105	0	$105

Your $305 check is honored, and you have $105 of Cash Reserve in use, for which you pay (at 12% per annum) only until your next deposit, thus:

Date	Checks	Deposits	Balance	Cash Reserve In Use
1/31			$200	0
2/5	$305	(CR) $205	0	$105
2/8		$350	$245	0

Therefore, you pay for the use of $105 for the three days only.

4. Next, compare with No. 2 above, when Cash Reserve is available:

Date	Checks	Deposits	Balance	Cash Reserve In Use
1/31			$200	0
2/4		$350	$550	0
2/5	$305		$245	0

Note that the $305 check clears your account, even though it is drawn against uncollected funds. The bank honors the check because it has given you a line of credit. If the $350 check you deposited to your account "bounces," the bank won't lose; it merely charges you back to the deposit date as if $105 of Cash Reserve had been in use.

Therefore, Cash Reserve enables the individual to draw immediately against a deposit, without concern for clearance time and at no cost to him. This may not appear to be of great importance, but it is, as will be demonstrated.

At this point, a word of caution is in order. All Cash Reserve-type services are not the same. Some may not automatically use your next deposit to reduce the Cash Reserve in use. Some will not place in Cash Reserve only the amount needed to cover a check, but will use multiples of $100. Some charge overdrafts automatically as a cash advance on your credit card—which means that excess money (earning no interest) may come into your checking account, which you are paying for as a cash advance. Still others may not honor checks drawn on uncollected funds, but will cover them with Cash Reserve, for which you pay.

The Chase Manhattan Bank's Cash Reserve Loan Service is one of the best we've seen and may be used as a standard against which other banks' services can be judged.

Cash Reserve features tied to one's checking account

eliminate the worry and cost of bouncing checks. It also makes it possible to draw against deposits without the delay of clearance time.

It also does much more. Some of what it can do for you is obvious, some will need explanation. Checks for end-of-month bills and taxes can be sent out on time, while the funds to cover the checks remain in a day of deposit to day of withdrawal account (or a money market fund-type account) for several days earning interest before it is necessary to transfer the funds to the checking account.

By doing this, a few days of extra interest is earned during bill-paying time. But isn't it a case of drawing checks against as yet undeposited funds, and isn't that something that should *never* be done? The answer is yes and no. It is a case of writing checks against undeposited funds, against an insufficient balance, but if a Cash Reserve has been arranged with the bank, it is not illegal! That is the purpose of Cash Reserve—to allow checks to be written in excess of the balance. Cash Reserve covers you until you deposit the money to cover the checks. If the deposit is made before the check comes back to the bank for clearance, it costs nothing. (See Fig. 13, which follows, Chase Manhattan's Cash Reserve.)

Cash Reserve Loan

It's an extension of your personal checking account. Cash Reserve gives you a personal line of credit from $500 to $5,000.

This means that extra money is always there when you need it. For emergencies. For shopping. For anything that comes up requiring cash. Or when it is a long time until payday.

If you need more money than you have in your checking account at the moment, you simply write a check. The extra money is automatically and immediately advanced. No negotiations; no approvals need-ed. However, you must live or work in the New York area to qualify. And, with your next checking account deposit, the balance you owe is automatically adjusted downwards.

Your Cash Reserve is always there when you need it, and it costs you nothing until you use it.

A Cash Reserve Loan lets you write checks for more than you have in your checking account. Now you can buy the things you need when you need them—even get immediate cash for emergencies without dipping into savings. It's the perfect extension of your checkbook balance.

Here's how it works

With Cash Reserve Checking, you command a personal line of credit from $500 to $5,000. You just write a check regardless of the amount on hand in your checking account. The Cash Reserve is always there. It costs you nothing until you use it. You never have to take money out of your savings account and lose the interest.

You simply write a check when you need it for the full amount of your balance *plus* the part of your Cash Reserve you need. This extra money is automatically advanced. No negotiations. No approvals. No bank signatures required. No red tape. And, with your next deposit, the balance you owe is automatically adjusted downwards.

Say, for example, that you need a washer and dryer that cost $397. Your checking account balance is only $100. You write the check for the full amount, and Chase immediately provides the needed $297 from your Cash Reserve. Your next checking account deposit will automatically reduce the balance you owe and replenish your Cash Reserve.

Lowest possible cost

Cash Reserve Checking is designed to keep the interest charges on your unpaid balances as low as possible.

Unlike the majority of overdraft checking plans, with Cash Reserve you pay interest only on the exact amount you use and only for the length of time you use it.

1. With Cash Reserve, you have money readily available and can keep your savings intact when you need emergency cash.

2. There are no charges for the Cash Reserve until you actually draw upon your reserve. You pay interest only on the exact amount of the Cash Reserve you use, and for the *exact* length of time you use it.

3. Each time you make a deposit in your Chase checking account, you automatically reduce any balance you owe, and at the same time replenish your Cash Reserve.

Fig. 13: Chase Manhattan's Cash Reserve (continued).

Although hundreds of banks give really free checking accounts, many levy a service charge if the average balance falls below, for example, $300 in any month. Here again, Cash Reserve can help if a savings account with a high balance is maintained at another bank.

As an example, assume that in some month the average balance will be about $125, or $175 below the minimum required to avoid a service charge of perhaps $3. Also assume that experience has shown that it takes two business days for a check deposited into the savings account to clear out of the checking account.

On Thursday write a check for $2,000 (backed by Cash
Reserve) and deposit it in the savings account. Assuming the
balance in the savings account exceeded $2,000 before the
deposit, withdraw from the savings account by teller's check
$2,000 drawn to your order. Deposit that $2,000 teller's check
into the checking account.

The balance in the savings account remains the same; $2,000
was deposited and $2,000 withdrawn.

The balance in the checking account increases by $2,000 until
the check you deposited into the savings account is returned to
your bank. Two business days after the Thursday transaction is
the following Monday. Because of the intervening weekend, the
checking account balance was increased by $2,000 for *four*
calendar days. That transaction, which cost nothing, increased
the checking average monthly balance by about $267, or more
than enough to make up the $175 deficit—more than enough to
avoid the service charge even if an almost zero balance had been
maintained. The checking account statement would appear
thus:

Date	Checks	Deposits	Balance	Cash Reserve In Use
Beg. of Mo.			$125	0
(Thursday)		$2,000	$2,125	0
(Monday)	$2,000		$125	0
End of Mo.			$125	0

It should now be obvious that Cash Reserve makes possible a
truly free checking account, even if the "free" account assesses
service charges when *average* balances fall below some
minimum.

For Mr. Alert, Cash Reserve permitted him to cover checks
he had used on the days he expected them to clear out of his account—without any concern that they may have been bounced.

Can Cash Reserve do anything for the person with a really free checking account or for those who keep sufficient balances to avoid service charges?

This time, let's combine a daily interest account having a balance of over $2,000 with the Cash Reserve/checking account. Assume the same clearance time as in the previous example, two business days.

As in the previous example, on Thursday write a check for $2,000 and deposit it into the savings account, but this time don't withdraw anything from the account. As before, Cash Reserve backs up the $2,000 check. On Monday, withdraw by cash or teller's check $2,000 from the savings account and deposit it to the checking account. The checking account statement would look something like this:

Date	Checks	Deposits	Balance	Cash Reserve In Use
			$444	0
(Monday)	$2,000	$2,000	$444	0

The daily interest savings passbook would appear like this:

Date	Withdrawals	Deposits	Balance
			$2,111
(Thursday)		$2,000	$4,111
(Monday)	$2,000		$2,111

The $2,000 would earn interest for four days, which, at 5¼%, amounts to $1.15. If $5,000 had been used instead of $2,000, the interest earned would amount to $2.88 for the one transaction.

If this would be done every other week for a year, or 26 times,

at an average annual rate of 5¼%, about $75 would be earned
—that is, $75 *more* than the normal interest on the $5,000 in the
savings account.

As of November 1, 1978, Federal regulations permit, and
banks are currently considering, ways to "cover" checks drawn
against uncollected or insufficient funds by automatically transferring funds out of one's savings account and into his checking
account. This, of course, amounts to just about the same as
New England's NOW accounts. However, when this service is
available, the service charge for each "coverage" may be steep
—and the interest terms on the applicable savings account may
be more restrictive than those of current day of deposit to day
of withdrawal accounts. Therefore, if the service is offered to
you, read the small print first!

Can You Spot the Loophole?

A forerunner of NOW (Negotiable Order of Withdrawal) was
an account described at the time as the "miracle" bank account
and officially known by its trademarked name, "United Security Account."

It was a highly successful combined checking and savings account which paid interest on savings, with no balances in the
checking account. However, people like our "Mr. Alert" quickly found that the account offered much more. The following
pages contain excerpts of the bank's advertising and instruc-
tional material. With the knowledge you have gained so far, can
you spot the money-making opportunity?

The reader is cautioned that although the account, in name,
may still be available today, the loophole, after remaining open
from about 1962 to 1972, was finally closed. A description of
this account is included to alert the reader to the type of
loophole one should watch for in bank advertising.

Now that you know there *is* a loophole, try to spot it yourself
without my help—and figure out how people earned a minimum

of 8% a year at a time when interest rates were much lower than they are today. Carefully follow the bank's ads and informational material.

Figure 14 shows the 1960's advertisement of the then unique type of account. The bank's public relations people described the account:

Announce Expansion of Only Bank Plan that

Allows Checks and Top Interest at Same Time

New Block of "U.S.A." Bank Accounts To Be Opened to the Public

Citizens Bank has announced that a new block of its "United Security Accounts" is being released to the public. These are the only bank accounts in the United States that pay maximum savings interest on money that would ordinarily be kept earning nothing in a checking account for immediate access. The interest is paid on all money deposited, yet accountholders can write free checks on credit against the entire account. There is no minimum balance required, no service or check charges. It can, in effect, be used like a completely free checking account without affecting the interest earned.

The bank is in the $100,000,000 class with exceptional reserves and full F.D.I.C. insurance. All transactions are by postage-free mail.

Although "U.S.A." accounts are held by some 30,000 depositors throughout the U.S., new accounts have only been available at limited, fixed intervals, mainly to persons recommended by current accountholders. Now the bank says it will release a block of new accounts for applicants without recommendation.

During this limited period, anyone interested is invited to send, without obligation, for a free booklet describing the advantages of these accounts. The coupon below should be sent without delay.

-------------- **FREE BOOKLET COUPON** --------------

Howard E. Hadley, U.S.A. Director
Citizens Bank & Trust Co.
(Park Ridge) Chicago, Ill. 60646

Please mail my Free Booklet with full information on how I can earn interest and write checks at the same time with your exclusive United Security Account plan.

Name _____

Address _____

City_____ State_____ Zip Code_____

CITIZENS BANK
& TRUST COMPANY

assets over $100,000,000.00

Fig. 14: Newspaper Advertisement for Unique Combined Savings-Checking Account.

"THE 'MIRACLE' BANK ACCOUNT"

It's the only one that works like a *checking account that pays interest* or a *savings account with checks*.

Most everyone has always wished he could get interest on his checking account, and most bankers would like to pay it, if it would expand their deposits. But every banker knows interest on demand (checking) deposits is absolutely impossible under the Federal Reserve Act as amended in 1933 and the Banking Act of 1935.

However, if you set up a line of check-credit against a savings account which naturally pays interest . . . and—*voila!*—you've done the impossible. That's just what happened several years ago when an enterprising Chicago suburban bank, Citizens Bank & Trust Co., in Park Ridge, Ill., came up with its "USA" account (United Security Account). Not surprisingly, the bank has been gathering tens of thousands of new depositors all over the world with tens of millions of new deposit dollars.

The workings of the USA account are remarkably simple: deposits are held as ordinary savings paying 4% interest (since this is the current maximum the Federal Reserve permits banks to pay). But "USA Cheques" can be written any time on the entire balance as collateral. All new deposits first repay the "cheque-loans" created, and the rest simply adds to the interest-earning savings balance.

According to Citizens' Roderick MacArthur, who invented the plan: "Many USA accountholders also use a separate checking account for day-to-day money, but they say this is the ideal place for 'in-between money'—the money you *might* need in cash at a moment's notice but don't want to leave idle until you do. It's the *only* place where this kind of money can earn any interest."

Some USA depositors keep large balances simply for the peace of mind they get from knowing it's always instantly available by check. Others use it for day-to-day checking by making routine deposits of salaries, receipts, etc. Theoretically, there's a ¾ %-per-month charge for the cheque-loans, but the routine deposits continuously "wash them out" during a free period up to 45 days before the charge is applied. Thus, they literally "do the impossible": earn interest on an account that works exactly like a regular checking account.

Although in the hundred-million-dollar class, Citizens Bank wasn't geared to handle the flood of deposits that poured in by mail from all over the country after the plan was first introduced. Standard procedures were too slow, posting machines couldn't do the unusual bookkeeping, and conversion to new equipment slowed things even more.

"It was a rough time," says MacArthur, "but it was a long time ago, and we learned our lesson."

The bank closed the door on new accounts, put the whole thing on magnetic tape with a new 501 computer, and cautiously opened the door again. MacArthur says it has been running like clockwork ever since.

USA accounts carry a unique guarantee in addition to all the standard ones: Whenever the Federal Reserve raises the interest ceiling, USA accounts are guaranteed in advance automatically to go to the new maximum no matter how high it is set. There is no minimum (or maximum) deposit limitation, checks are 15¢, and all other free account services are included.

(Editor's Note: As of January 1970, Federal Reserve raised the interest ceiling on savings accounts from 4% to 4½%.)

When the coupon shown in Figure 14 (pg. 67) was sent in to the bank, the materials shown in Figures 15 and 16 (pgs. 71, 72) were returned together with account-opening forms. Read these two pieces carefully to see if you can spot the way to use the account for extra profit.

UNITED SECURITY ACCOUNT
DIVISION OF
CITIZENS BANK & TRUST COMPANY
CHICAGO, ILLINOIS 60648

Dear Friend:

Thank you for asking about a United Security Account.

I'm happy to tell you I can set aside an account for you. To take advantage of it, please return the validated application form with your deposit of $10.00 or more within 10 days. A second form is enclosed for your records.

If I do not hear from you in 10 days we will have to reassign your account. It is the only way we can be fair to the many applicants.

The United Security Account is the ONLY bank account in the entire United States that does both at once: Lets you earn the highest rate of interest on your savings, yet write checks whenever you want.

The mechanics are not complicated: The checks you write are simply loans. If you repay them with a new deposit by the middle of the following month, there is no charge. If you don't, there is a charge of ½% per month until you do -- but remember, the money behind every check you write also continues to earn you full interest. In other words, all the money in your account earns full guaranteed interest, no matter how many checks you write. The checks are 15¢, and everything else is free.

The United Security Account plan has been carefully tested and proved over seven years under stringent governmental controls. Please read the enclosed folder now to see how thousands of other accountholders from coast to coast are truly "having their cake and eating it too" -- earning full interest on money which in effect remains in their pocket in the form of U.S.A. Cheques. Many of them also like the advantages of a convenient, confidential, out-of-town account.

Read how easy it is to combine the high interest earnings and checking privileges you get with no other account...anywhere. Then use the airmail envelope -- we pay postage both ways on all transactions. And please don't forget the 10-day time limit.

Meanwhile, if you have any questions, please write me. I look forward to serving you -- both personally and on behalf of Citizens Bank.

Sincerely yours,

Howard S Hadley

HOWARD S. HADLEY
Director of Division

Fig. 15: Information about the United Security Account.

A NOTE ON "UNCOLLECTED FUNDS"

If your United Security Account Cheque Credit Available ever gets so low that your next U.S.A. Cheque will be against the credit of your last deposit, it's best to make sure this deposit is eight business-days old (for deposit checks drawn on other banks in the United States) or older. If your deposit is in checks on banks in a foreign country, it is best to wait up to twenty business days, depending on the country, before writing your U.S.A. Cheque. (You do not have to count time for your deposits or cheques to get to this bank because the time each takes will be about the same).

This does not mean your deposits are not credited immediately for earning U.S.A. interest or repaying Cheque-loans. It simply means that for writing checks, this bank, like every other bank in the United States, only accepts deposits "subject to collection"; that is, subject to their actually being paid by the other banks on which the checks are drawn. Until then they are "uncollected funds".

We do, however, make exceptions for U.S. Accounts: If your deposit is in "official" checks -- money order, payroll, cashier's, or government checks, etc., -- you can safely write a U.S.A. Cheque against it right away. But the safest thing is simply to keep enough balance in your account so that your next cheque will not depend on your last deposit. In any ordinary checking account, this balance might be "dead". But in your U.S. Account, it not only lets you write cheques on "collected funds", it automatically earns more interest money for you.

UNITED SECURITY ACCOUNT DIVISION

Fig. 16: Uncollected Funds and the United Security Account.

See the chance for profit? If you're stumped, here is a hint: While daily interest accounts pay interest to day of withdrawal, the USA account offered to pay interest even *after* withdrawal —for 15 to 45 days. At first glance, this may not sound like a big deal, but that interest, plus daily interest accounts properly used, yielded upward of 8%—and even as high as 18%—at a time when interest rates were materially lower than they are today.

Another hint: Read again the last eight lines in Figure 16 (page 72) on "official checks."

If the answer is still not clear, there follows an example of how the account had been used for profit.

A USA account had been previously opened with a nominal deposit of $10 (Account #1). In addition, another account (Account #2) had been opened at a local savings and loan association paying 5% (DD-DW) and paying interest from the 1st of the month on deposits made by the 10th if kept in the account until the end of the quarter.

Recap

Account #1—USA account

Account #2—DD-DW a/c in S&L (with deposits made by the 10th to earn interest from the 1st).

1. Using a teller's check, or other instrument acceptable as cash (see Fig. 16), deposit $10,000 into Account #1 on October 2nd, by mailing early on October 1st. (In the mid-'60s, the U.S. Post Office was more dependable than it is today.)

2. On October 3rd, draw a $10,000 USA check on Account #1 and deposit this check into the local S&L Account #2. (Note that this USA check is not an instrument acceptable as cash at any bank. By the rules of the S&L into which it is deposited, as much as 20 days may be required for it to clear.)

3. On November 3rd, withdraw from Account #2 $10,000.15 by teller's check made out to yourself. Endorse and mail this check as a deposit to Account #1.

(On or about November 5th, the bank statement for October with cancelled check will have been received for Account #1, showing a check-loan of $10,000 outstanding and a service charge of 15¢. By having sent the deposit of $10,000.15 in step 3, the check-loan of $10,000 was repaid and the 15¢ service charge paid. This deposit, as repayment of loan, is recorded upon receipt into Account #1 on or about November 4th.)

4. On November 5th, draw a $10,000 USA check to yourself and deposit it into Account #2 (same procedure as in step 2).

5. On December 1st, by teller's check, withdraw $10,000.15 from Account #2 and mail it for deposit into Account #1 (same as step 3).

6. On December 10th, repeat step 4, by depositing your USA check for $10,000 into Account #2.

[Note that steps 1, 3, and 5 required a trip to the local S&L (Account #2); steps 2, 4, and 6 required writing and mailing checks for deposit into Account #1, using prepaid mailers supplied by the bank.]

At the time of the above example, commercial banks could pay only 4½% interest, savings institutions 5%. Ten thousand dollars deposited at 4½% would have earned $112.50, while at 5%, $125 would have been earned. The example above provided a yield of 9.2%, equal to $230. Here is how it is computed:

A. Account #1 earned interest on $10,000 for the entire quarter at 4½% to a total of $112.50. Three separate times sums of $10,000 were borrowed against the collateral of the

USA account, but each time the loan was repaid prior to the 15th of the month following the loan, so the loan was free of any interest charges. Fifteen cents was paid for each of the three checks used, so Account #1 earned $112.50—less 45¢ in check charges—to a net of $112.05. (The 15¢ check charge was later dropped by the bank.)

B. Account #2 earned interest on $10,000 on the following dates:

> (1) October 3rd through November 3rd = 31 days
> (2) November 5th through December 31st = 57 days
> (The December 10th deposit earned interest from December 1st because the $10,000 remained in the account until the end of the quarter.)

The interest earned in Account #2 was for 88 of the 92 days in the quarter, or, at 5%, approximately $118.

C. Therefore, interest earned from October 1st through December 31st was $112 (Account #1) plus $118 (Account #2) to a total of $230, equal to an annual rate of 9.2%.

It should be noted that steps 1 through 6 in the preceding example were accomplished by using the advantages of both accounts in accordance with the rules in effect at that time. However, it is evident that the bank lost money on every USA account holder who used the account solely for the purpose of earning double interest. It is probable that too many people took this advantage, thereby influencing the bank to change its regulations for all account holders. If only a few had exploited the loophole, it is possible that the original regulations would still be in effect. The history of the USA account should be a strong argument for keeping one's mouth shut about loopholes—once the general public is aware of them, banks quickly close them.

However, if banking loopholes are not publicized, how can

you, the reader, learn about them? Find them for yourself, use them, and keep them to yourself! From the knowledge you already have, you will find it is easy to spot both loopholes and pitfalls. There follows a current example of both—with an explanation of how to analyze a bank's offerings.

In mid-1977, one of the largest banks in the country, the innovative bank that popularized day of deposit to day of withdrawal accounts, Chase-Manhattan, opened a "Chase Savings Center" at every one of its hundreds of branches. Following are excerpts from "A Review of Chase Savings Programs," published by Chase and dated June 1977:

Together, you and the Chase Savings Advisor can: Review your present savings plans, establish savings goals that meet your needs, evaluate the alternate savings programs offered by Chase, select your savings program. In this booklet you have a review of the wide variety of savings programs that Chase can offer you. Your Chase Savings Advisor will be pleased to discuss each of these savings plans, and to assist you in selecting the ones that are best for you and your goals.

Your Savings Advisor can also show you how to combine savings with all of your banking needs: free checking, cash reserve, instalment loans, safe deposit, Visa® Card (formerly BankAmericard®), and more. At Chase, you have more than 200 locations to do your savings and banking conveniently.

Chase Interest-In-Advance Savings Plan*

Collect your interest in advance—when you open your account.** With a new Chase Advance Interest Savings Certificate, you can receive up to 10 years interest—in advance—when you open your account. Your interest is the highest prepaid interest allowed by law, and the rate will vary depending on how long you agree to leave your deposit in the Bank—anywhere from one to ten years. This way you have all your interest in advance, without the risk that it will be diminished by inflation. Meantime, your savings principal remains intact in your Time Deposit Account, and comes to you in full at maturity.

---

*Federal law and regulation prohibit the payment of a time deposit prior to maturity, or stated withdrawal periods, unless three months of the interest thereon is forfeited and interest on the amount withdrawn is reduced to the passbook rate.

**Your prepaid interest is subject to income taxes in the year in which the interest is paid.

For example, if you invest $1,000 in a three-year Savings Certificate, you immediately receive $172.15 in full interest when you make your deposit. And, at the end of three years, your $1,000 is returned to you in full. Your Chase Savings Advisor can show you how your Interest-In-Advance can be even higher if you select a longer term plan, and also other ways to use this new Chase Advantage.

A Chase High Growth Savings Bond*

This new bond pays more than Uncle Sam's! For example, for only $4,673.71 you can buy a Chase High Growth Savings Bond that you can cash in for $10,000 in just 10 years.

Chase High Growth Savings Bonds are also available in denominations of $1,000 to $100,000. And they pay the highest interest allowed by law—from 6.0% to 7.5% depending on maturity. So decide now how much you'd like to have for the future. Then make sure you will have it by buying the Chase High Growth Savings Bond you need.

7.50% Nest Egg*

Provides 7.50% interest compounded daily for an effective yield of 7.90%. Available from a minimum balance of $1,000 to a maximum balance of $50,000. Offered with 6 to 10-year maturity dates and may be automatically renewable.

7.25% Nest Egg*

Provides 7.25% interest compounded daily for an effective annual yield of 7.63%. Available from a minimum balance of $1,000 to a maximum balance of $50,000. Offered with 4 to 6-year maturity dates and may be automatically renewable.

6.50% Nest Egg*

Provides 6.50% interest compounded daily for an effective annual yield of 6.81%. Available from a minimum balance of $500 to a maximum balance of $100,000. Offered with 2½ to 10-year maturity dates and may be automatically renewable.

6.00% Nest Egg*

Provides 6.00% interest compounded daily for an effective annual yield of 6.27%. Available from a minimum balance of $500 to a maximum balance of $100,000. Offered with 1 to 2½-year maturity dates, and may be automatically renewable.

5.50% Regular Nest Egg*

Provides 5.50% interest compounded daily for an effective annual

---

Federal law and regulation prohibit the payment of a time deposit prior to maturity, or stated withdrawal periods, unless three months of the interest thereon is forfeited and interest on the amount withdrawn is reduced to the passbook rate.

yield of 5.73%. Available from a minimum balance of $500 to a max-imum balance of $100,000. Offered as a 90-Day Notice Account and will automatically renew every calendar quarter. WITHDRAWALS: You may make withdrawals at any time by giving us 90 days written notice and you will continue to receive 5.50% interest during that time. You may also, in the absence of any written notice, make withdrawals dur-ing the first 10 days of every January, April, July and October and in-terest will be paid on the amount withdrawn to the first day of such month, provided money has been on deposit for 90 days through the first day of the quarter.

5.00% Regular Passbook Savings

Provides 5.00% interest compounded and credited quarterly. Every dollar that you deposit earns interest from the day of deposit to the day of withdrawal, providing only that a $5 balance remains in your ac-count to the end of the quarter.

You may make additional deposits as frequently as you would like to. Any deposit you make up to the tenth day of any quarter will earn in-terest from the first day of that quarter. Any amounts withdrawn dur-ing the last three business days of a quarter will earn interest to the end of that quarter.

5.00% Statement Savings

It is also possible to save at Chase without a passbook. Chase offers statement savings at 5.00% interest, and eliminates the need for a passbook entirely. You don't need a passbook to make deposits or withdrawals. You don't have to bring your passbook into the Bank to have your interest posted each quarter. And you don't need to worry about losing your passbook.

You get a complete record of all your savings activity in one conven-ient, easy-to-understand, quarterly statement. This statement will be mailed to either your home or office every three months and will list all deposits, withdrawals, and all interest earned during that quarter.

Having read the brochure excerpts once, it might be well worth it to re-read them more carefully. Have you noticed anything unusual? Let's start with the Interest In Advance Sav-ings Plan and the footnote, "Your prepaid interest . . . is paid."

On the surface of it, you invest $1,000 for three years, you receive $172.15 in interest now (in advance), and you pay in-come taxes on the $172.15 as this year's income. This tax feature might be beneficial to someone whose income is low this year, but expects his income to be substantially larger during the next three years. (For example, someone starting a new business might expect losses the first year but profits thereafter. Or a writer, working on a book to be published the following year.) In such a case it may be profitable to pay taxes in advance—at the lower rates.

Looking at this plan from another viewpoint, you are investing $1,000 *minus* $172.15, or $827.85 for three years, will pay income tax on $172.15, and will collect $1,000 three years from now. Isn't this, in effect, the same as depositing $827.85 into a three-year term certificate, the only difference being that taxes on interest are paid in one year instead of over a period of three or four years? Have you stopped to figure what interest *rate* you are getting for this three-year term deposit?

First, look at the description of the "6.50% Nest Egg." It states that "6.50% interest compounded daily [gives] an effective annual yield of 6.81%."

With the "Interest in Advance" account, as just shown, a net investment of $827.85 becomes $1,000 in three years. Let us see what happens if the same $827.85 is put into the 6.50% account that yields 6.81% annually.

To compute compound interest, the following formula is used:

$$CA = (1 + i)^n \times P \text{ where}$$

CA	=	Compound Amount (principal and interest)
i	=	Interest Rate (expressed as a decimal)
n	=	Number of Years interest is compounded
P	=	Principal (on deposit earning interest)

In this example,

i	=	.0681 (6.81% annual yield)
n	=	3 (years)
P	=	$827.85

Therefore,

$$CA = (1 + .0681)^3 \times \$827.85$$
$$= (1.0681)^3 \times \$827.85$$
$$= 1.0681 \times 1.0681 \times 1.0681 \times \$827.85$$

Multiplying by hand or using your electronic calculator, we find, CA = \$1,008.76.

That is \$8.76 more than the "Interest in Advance" account yields.

We have read that the "6.50% Nest Egg" account yields 6.81% because the 6.50% is compounded daily. Just for the fun of it, let us find out what the compound amount will be on \$827.85 at 6.50% compounded annually (not daily), thereby giving an annual yield of 6.50% instead of 6.81%.

$$CA = (1 + i)^n \times P$$
$$= (1.065)^3 \times \$827.85$$
$$= 1.065 \times 1.065 \times 1.065 \times \$827.85$$
$$= \$1,000.00 \; ! \; ! \; !$$

So we see that the 6.50% Nest Egg account gives an annual yield of 6.81%, while the Interest in Advance account yields only 6.50%.

But don't blame the bank; Federal regulations prevent their paying more than the nominal maximum interest rate on this type of account.

And don't summarily discard the Interest in Advance accounts. Though the earnings may be slightly less (\$172.15 as compared to \$180.91 on \$827.85 for three years), tax savings under special circumstances, as previously described, could be much more than the slight loss of interest.

What was learned about the Interest in Advance Savings Plan

may be of little consequence to most people, but it points up the importance of reading between the lines to ascertain what drawbacks or advantages may be hidden. It is not told to you—even in small print.

For a few moments, let us leave the review of Chase Savings Programs to make note of a novel bank offering. A nationally circulated business newspaper carried the story of the Washington, D.C. Bank of Columbia's offer of a Mercedes Benz 450 SL or $27,000 in cash as *advance interest* in return for a deposit of $65,000 for seven years or $400,000 for one year. According to *The New York Times* (datelined July 15, 1978—UPI), in 24 hours the bank received 128 telephone inquiries and three promises of deposits.

People with that kind of money should be sufficiently sophisticated to grab a good deal when they see one—or reject a bad one. Were you in a position to, would you take the deal? Let us dissect it.

First: A $27,000 car or $27,000 cash for a $65,000 deposit for seven years.

If you take the car, what you are actually doing is depositing $38,000 for seven years *and* buying a car for $27,000 (total = $65,000). *And* you will pay income taxes in one year (1978) on $27,000—reported as advance interest.

If you opt for the cash $27,000 interest in advance, you are depositing $38,000 for seven years—*and* you will pay income taxes on the $27,000 as advance interest.

And your $38,000 deposit will grow to $65,000 in seven years.

Now let us compare this growth with what is generally available across the country.

Recall that Chase-Manhattan's "Interest in Advance" account for three years paid at the rate of 6.50% (see pg. 80).

Interest for seven years would be at the rate of 7.50%. Let us compare this with Columbia's offer.

$$CA = (1 + i)^n \times P \text{ (see pg. 79)}$$
$$CA = (1 + .075)^7 \times \$38,000$$
$$CA = \$63,043.87 - \text{(compared to \$65,000 at Columbia)}$$

Discarding the "interest in advance" feature, commercial banks (including Chase) offer 7½% compounded to yield 7.90% on six- to seven-year term deposits. Using the interest tables (see pg. 137), we determine that $38,000 in seven years grows to $64,704.39 (as compared to $65,000 from the Bank of Columbia's offer). (Interest was computed as follows: $10,000 at 7½%, compounded to yield 7.90%, for seven years grows to $17,027.47. Thirty-eight thousand dollars is 3.8 times as much as $10,000. Therefore, the Compound Amount on $38,000 is 3.8 times as much as on $10,000, or $17,027.47 × 3.8 = $64,704.39.)

Since this amount, $64,704.39, is the most "allowed by law" to be paid by a commercial bank that is a member of the Federal Reserve System and/or insured by the F.D.I.C., we must wonder how the Bank of Columbia can offer $65,000.

Savings banks and associations can and do offer 7¾%, yielding 8.17% for the same term. Thirty-eight thousand dollars grows to $65,846.29. (From the table on page 138, a yield of 8.17% on $10,000 for seven years gives the sum of $17,327.97. This amount multiplied by 3.8 gives a total of $65,846.29.) The additional $846.29 of earned interest, compared to Columbia's interest, should be enough to pay for a stop at your friendly Mercedes service station.

It should be noted that if the $38,000 is deposited for eight years (instead of seven), the interest rate jumps to 8% and the yield to 8.45%, so that the $38,000 *after seven years* is worth $67,048.72, or $2,048.72 more than with Columbia's offer.

And for tax purposes, the interest is spread over a seven- or eight-year period—probably at lower tax rates than $27,000 added to your income in one year!

Next: Should anyone sitting with $400,000 in ready cash fall for Columbia's one-year promotion?

In this case, $400,000 minus $27,000 advance interest is the same as a deposit of $373,000 which grows to $400,000 in one year.

Principal × Rate × Time = Interest   or

P × R × T = I

$373,000 × Rate × 1 (year) = $27,000

$$\text{Rate} = \frac{\$27,000}{\$373,000} = 7.24\%$$

On deposits of $100,000 or more, banks can offer any interest rate they wish, unrestricted by the regulations of the Federal Reserve Board, FDIC, or FSLIC. As of July 1978, anyone wanting to deposit $373,000 in one bank for one year (with only $40,000 of it federally insured) could negotiate a rate of between 8% and 9% and choose a bank with assets in the billions as compared to Columbia's $47 million. By the end of '78 and into early '79, the rates jumped to between 10% and 12%.

Now let us return to the review of Chase Savings Programs to uncover a blooper as well as a highly unusual money-making opportunity.

In the description of the various Nest Egg Plans, Chase states that 7.50% compounded *daily* yields 7.90%, 7.25% yields 7.63%, 6.50% yields 6.81%, 6.00% yields 6.27% and 5.50% yields 5.73%. Actually, the yields given are for *continuous* compounding, not daily compounding. See Table I, page 127, for the correct yields when these nominal interest rates are compounded daily as well as continuously.

Now, on to the two small paragraphs under "5.00% Regular Passbook Savings."

If by this time you are really discerning, the first paragraph should pose an immediate question which needs answering. The second paragraph should make you do a double take.

The question about the first paragraph is simple. The 5.00% Regular Passbook Savings "provides 5.00% interest compounded and credited *quarterly*." The five "Nest Egg" accounts provide for interest compounded *daily*, and state the effective annual yield for each. What is the effective annual yield of 5.00% compounded quarterly? To compute this we use the formula:

$$EY = (1 + \tfrac{i}{n/y})^{n/y} - 1 \qquad \text{where}$$

EY = Effective Annual Yield

   i = annual rate of interest, expressed as a decimal
        (5.00% = .0500)

n/y = number of times interest is compounded per year.
        (For quarterly compounding, n/y = 4)

$$EY(1 + \tfrac{.05}{4})^4 - 1$$

$$= 1.0125^4 - 1$$

$$= (1.0125 \times 1.0125 \times 1.0125 \times 1.0125) - 1$$

$$= 1.050945337 - 1 = .0509$$

$$= 5.09\%$$

So, 5% compounded quarterly yields 5.09% annually. (Daily compounding would yield 5.13%—not much difference.)

Now to the second paragraph describing the 5.00% Regular Passbook Savings Account. It is reprinted below. Do you notice anything unusual?

> You may make additional deposits as frequently as you would like to. Any deposit you make up to the tenth day of any quarter will earn interest from the first day of that quarter. Any amounts withdrawn during the last three business days of a quarter will earn interest to the end of that quarter.

If the loophole still is not evident to you, compare the paragraph to descriptions of other institutions' savings accounts. A sample is printed for comparison. (Fig. 17, pg. 86.)

1. Note that both accounts offer interest from day of deposit to day of withdrawal (DD-DW).

2. West Side (Fig. 17, pg. 86) offers 10 grace days every month. Chase offers them only in January, April, July, and October.

3. One requires a minimum balance of $5, the other has no such requirement.

4. West Side pays 5.25% yielding 5.47%; Chase pays 5.00% with a yield of 5.09%.

So far, it *appears* that neither offers anything unusual—and West Side looks better than Chase. Yet the Chase account, depending on how it is used, makes possible increasing Mr. Alert's (see pgs. 48-55) double interest days by 11 each quarter, or short-term yields at an annual rate of 8.10%, 10.00%, 10.56%, 11.25%, 12.14%, 13.33%, 15.00%, 17.50%, 21.67%, and even 30.00% and 55.00%!

If you still have not spotted the loophole, here it is:

> Remember, Mr. Alert's savings account at a savings bank offered 10 grace days every month, but funds had to remain in the account until the end of the quarter to earn interest. Only regular savings

**DAY-OF-DEPOSIT-TO-DAY-OF-WITHDRAWAL
PACE SETTER**

SAVINGS
ACCOUNTS —
5.47% EFFECTIVE ANNUAL YIELD ON   5.25% PER ANNUM CURRENT RATE COMPOUNDED DAILY AND CREDITED QUARTERLY

**Pace Setter Savings Accounts earn the highest
legal passbook rate paid by any financial
institution PLUS:**

- Interest is compounded daily from day of
  deposit to day of withdrawal!
- You earn more than the stated effective
  rate of interest because we offer in the same
  account up to 10 Extra Interest Days every
  month — deposits made by the 10th earn
  interest from the 1st, provided they remain
  to the end of the quarter!
- No minimum balance is required!
- West Side returns the highest annual yield
  available when principal and interest remain
  in your account for a full year!

**NO BANK IN NEW YORK CITY OFFERS ALL
THESE FEATURES IN THE SAME PASSBOOK
ACCOUNT!**

**IT'S LIKE AN INTEREST-
EARNING CHECKING ACCOUNT!**

Make withdrawals as often as you like. You'll
never lose a single day's interest. And there's
never a penalty for withdrawing funds.

IDEAL FOR CORPORATE ACCOUNTS

By law no bank in New York may offer this type
of account to corporate depositors — but
West Side can! So use a 5.47% West Side
Federal Pace Setter Savings Account to invest
pension funds, accumulate tax payments or
earn extra dollars on excess corporate cash.
In any money market this account is always a
sound business or corporate investment.

Fig. 17: West Side Federal S&L Account Features.

accounts (Reg. a/c) gave the grace days; DD-DW accounts did not.

The West Side Federal S&L account combined the benefits of both accounts, offering interest from day of deposit to day of withdrawal (DD-DW) *plus* 10 grace days every month—*provided the funds so deposited remain in the account until the end of the quarter.*

However, Chase has no such restriction. Reread the second paragraph. "Any deposit you make up to the tenth day of any quarter (January 10, April 10, July 10, October 10) will earn interest from the first day of that quarter." Period. There is no requirement that deposits made up to the 10th remain for *any period whatsoever* in order to earn from the 1st.

Several people checked this conclusion with their friends at Chase-Manhattan. Not only was it confirmed that Chase means what it says, but one of the Chase Savings Advisors confided that his brother made good use of the extremely liberal grace days allowance.

And if you are unable to figure out for yourself just how profitable the 5.00% Regular Passbook Savings account can be, following are detailed some ideas.

First, let us go back to Mr. Alert. Remember, he had two accounts at a commercial bank. Let's suppose his commercial bank was Chase (or any other bank that might be offering the same grace-day rule as Chase-Manhattan does on its 5.00% Regular Passbook Savings account).

Recap

Commercial Bank	Savings Bank
1. CB/Check a/c	3. SB/Check a/c
2. CB/DD-DW a/c	4. SB/DD-DW a/c
	5. SB/Reg. a/c

March 1978

Sun	Mon	Tue	Wed	Thu	Fri	Sat
			1	2	3	4
5	6	7	8	9	10	11
12	13	14	15	16	17	18
19	20	21	22	23	24	25
26	27	28	29	30	31	

April 1978

Sun	Mon	Tue	Wed	Thu	Fri	Sat
						1
2	3	4	5	6	7	7
9	10	11	12	13	14	15
16	17	18	19	20	21	22
23	24	25	26	27	28	29
30						

Recall that Mr. Alert made the following deposits and withdrawals:

Step 1. (Friday, after 3 P.M., 3/10). Transfer $10,000 from Account #2 to Account #1. (Effective date is 3/13.)

Step 2. (Friday evening, 3/10). Write check on Account #1 for $10,000 and deposit it into Account #5.

Step 3. (3/29, 3/30, or 3/31). Transfer $10,000 from Account #5 to Account #4.

(The result of Steps 1 and 2 was that double interest was earned during the first 13 days of March. Step 3 provided for daily interest on and after April 1.)

Here is how Mr. Alert can continue earning double interest for the first 11 days of April:

Step 4. (Monday, 4/10, *before 3 P.M.). Write check for $10,000 on Account #3* and deposit it into Account #2.

Step 5. (Tuesday, 4/11). Transfer $10,000 from Account #4 to Account #3.

(The result of Step 4 is that $10,000 earns interest in Account #2 from 4/1 while Step 5 covers the check written in Step 4 and interest is earned in Account #4 through 4/11. Thus, double interest is earned during the first 11 days of April.)

The example of Mr. Alert shows that interest at the (annualized) rate of 10¼% was earned the first 13 days of March and the first 11 days of April. Or, from March 1st through April 11th (42 days), interest at the rate of 5¼% was earned, *plus* interest at 5% for 24 days—for a combined yield of 8.1%.

And now the reader may understand why Mr. Alert did not bother to take advantage of the three bonus days at the end of March, as previously described on pages 48 through 55.

Anyone who knows about interest rates on long-term investments, including six to seven and eight to 10-year term certificates may wonder why one as astute as Mr. Alert would go through all the effort required to earn 8.1% when 7.75% certificates (yielding 8.17%), and 8.0% certificates (yielding 8.45%) are available. Mr. Alert, and others like him, have a couple of good reasons.

First, no matter how large one's estate may be, some of the funds should be kept liquid—readily available for emergencies or opportunities. Second, money market interest rates can and do change radically from year to year and even month to month. As an example, a few years ago and for a period lasting more than a year, short-term interest rates of 12% and more were available through the money market funds—but only if the investor had liquid funds available.

Likewise, long-term interest rates vary. In 1975 and early 1976, savings certificate rates were as high as 7.75%, yielding 8.17%. (See Fig. 18A, pg. 90.) In the latter part of 1976, most

banks dropped their rates to a maximum of 7.00%, yielding
7.35%. (See Fig. 18B, below.) It was not until June 1977 that
many banks went back to their previous 7.75% rate. And, finally, on June 1, 1978, eight to 10-year certificates yielding 8.45%
on the nominal rate of 8.0% were permitted on deposits of
$1,000 or more. (See Fig. 18C, pg. 91.)

THE BOWERY SAVINGS BANK
Interest and Dividend Rates

INVESTMENT SAVINGS ACCOUNTS

Guaranteed Annual Interest Rate	Effective Annual Yield	Minimum Deposit	Term
7.75%	8.17%	$1000	6-7 years
7.50%	7.90%	$1000	4-6 years
6.75%	7.08%	$ 500	2½-4 years
6.50%	6.81%	$ 500	1-2½ years
5.75%	6.00%	$ 500	90-364 days

**Fig. 18A: Interest rates in 1975 through early 1976 These rates
were again available in mid-1977.**

The East New York
Savings Bank

(Effective December 15, 1976)

	RATE PER ANNUM	YIELD	MINIMUM DEPOSIT
Regular Savings Account	5¼%	5.47%	$1.00
Day-of-Deposit/ Day-of-Withdrawal Account	5¼%	5.47%	$1.00
Time Deposit Account: 5-7 years	7%	7.35%	$1000
2½-5 years	6½%	6.81%	$500
1-2½ years	6%	6.27%	$500

Fig. 18B: Lowered interest rates, December 1976.

GUARANTEED TIME DEPOSIT ACCOUNTS

8.45% is the effective annual yield on **8.00%**
8 year or longer Time Deposit Accounts.
Minimum deposit: $1,000.

8.17% is the effective annual yield on **7.75%**
6 to 7 year Time Deposit Accounts. Minimum deposit: $1,000.

7.90% is the effective annual yield on **7.50%**
4 to 6 year Time Deposit Accounts. Minimum deposit: $1,000.

7.08% is the effective annual yield on **6.75%**
2½ to 4 year Time Deposit Accounts. Minimum deposit: $500.

6.81% is the effective annual yield on **6.50%**
14 month to 2½ year Time Deposit Accounts.
Minimum deposit: $500.

Note: Premature withdrawal on Time Deposit Accounts, if permitted by the bank, will result in the imposition of a Substantial Penalty.

Fig. 18C: Increased interest rates, June 1978.

In building an estate and making it grow, many people feel it is a good idea to keep available in liquid funds at least enough money to cover living expenses for three to six months. However, if such a sum is just left in a savings account, on average, one's estate will end up about $50,000 poorer—as will be explained in a later chapter. So, although it is generally well to keep some funds liquid, to keep from being so much poorer it is essential that every trick in the book be used to increase the return on idle funds to as much as possible. If liquid funds in excess of $10,000 are kept, the varying rate on minimum $10,000 six-month certificates should be watched—and compared to yields available through other short-term means.

Some people are in the fortunate position of being able to

make short-term, relatively safe loans at high interest rates of from 12% to 20%. The following example of what an accountant has been doing to maintain a good income on his liquid funds demonstrates how high rates, even though they are available for short periods only, can result in respectable overall average earnings.

The CPA, in private practice, has a number of small retail store clients. In general, their bills must be paid by the 30th of the month following their receipt of merchandise. Trade practices permit the retailer to take a discount if bills are paid by the 10th of the month, with the discounts ranging from 2% to 8%, depending upon the industry. "2/10 EOM" indicates that a 2% discount can be taken on items paid by the 10th of the month following the invoice date, while "2/10 NET 30" means that the bill must be paid within 10 days of the invoice date in order to earn the 2% discount.

Several times during a year a store may be short of cash with which to pay bills on the 10th. Paying bills at the end of the month, thereby losing the cash discount, is costly. If the discount is 2%, for a delay of 20 days from the 10th to the 30th, the store pays the equivalent of more than 36% interest.

Example

$10,000 less 2% = $9,800, payable 4/10
$10,000 net = $10,000, payable 4/30
Therefore, the cost of $9,800 for 20 days (10th to 30th) is $200, equivalent to about 37¼% annual interest.

During the first "money crunch" in 1965-66 when business found it almost impossible to borrow money from banks, the accountant, as a service to his clients, enlisted the help of two friends, and together they pooled their liquid funds for the purpose of making short-term loans to clients in need of cash with which to take discounts. They started with about $35,000 and over the years increased their pool to $120,000.

In addition to helping his clients, the accountant figured that he had an excellent way of keeping his liquid savings earning as much as, or more than, they would from long-term investments. When the money was not in use, it was kept in a few savings accounts earning the minimal 5% or 5¼%. Some of the time, part or all of the funds were out on loans earning from 12% to 18%, depending on the money market rates at the time. Between the two, they expected to average about 9%. Their risk was minimal. The accountant knew the financial condition of his clients and would, therefore, make loans only to those he felt strongly would not default.

Experience showed that many of their loans were made not necessarily on the 10th of the month, but on the 11th, 12th, and through the 15th, because some of the storekeepers took advantage of float in the payment of their bills and, therefore, did not borrow money to cover checks until the checks were returned for collection.

This resulted in the CPA's group making loans for an average of less than the full 20 days, which decreased their income. To compensate for some of the loss, they did much the same as Mr. Alert had done with savings account balances. Then they became aware of Chase's policy on 5.00% Regular Passbook Savings accounts, and their problem was solved. They figured that during four months of the year the following could be accomplished:

A. 12% to 18% could be earned on monies loaned out for the periods of the loans (the latter part of the months).

B. On monies loaned out after the 10th and through the 15th of the month, 9.2% to 10.7% could be earned from the 1st through the date the loan would be made.

C. On monies not loaned out that month, 6.9% (instead of 5% or 5¼%) could be earned.

D. Average earnings for those months would probably exceed 10%.

Following is an example of how these rates could be achieved:

Assume that $70,000 is in one or two DD-DW ac-
counts as of April 1, earning 5¼%. On each of the six
days from 4/10 through 4/15, $10,000 is loaned out
until the end of the month at between 12% and 18%,
to a total of $60,000. Ten thousand dollars remains
unused, not needed for loans. For simplicity,
weekends are assumed to be business days. (It should
be noted that the accountant is a good customer of
the banks involved, having savings certificates, checking, trust and custodial accounts at the banks, and in
addition, at Chase, maintaining his business checking
account. In general, commercial banks are particularly cooperative with lawyers and accountants because
of the business they bring into banks.)

A (1) On April 10th, a check(s) for $70,000 is written on
the savings bank checking account and deposited into the Chase 5.00% account.

A (2) On April 10th, using Chase check(s), $10,000 is
loaned out.

B (3) On April 11th, $70,000 is transferred from the sav-
ings bank DD-DW account(s) to the checking ac-
count(s) (at the same bank) to cover the check(s)
issued in A (1) above.

B (4) On April 11th, at Chase, $10,000 is transferred from
the 5.00% account to the checking account to cover
check(s) issued in A (2) above.

B (5) On April 11th (using Chase checks), $10,000 is
loaned out.

C (6) On April 12th, 13th, 14th, 15th, and 16th, step B (4)
above is repeated each day.

C (7) On April 12th, 13th, 14th, and 15th, step B (5) above is repeated each day.

Summary

1. On 4/10, $70,000 is deposited into the Chase 5.00% a/c (withdrawn from the DD-DW a/c on 4/11).

2. On the six days—from 4/10 through 4/15—$10,000 in loans are dispersed each day, to a total of $60,000 invested in short-term loans.

3. On the six days—from 4/11 through 4/16—$10,000 each day is transferred from the 5.00% a/c to the checking a/c to cover check(s) dispersed in 2 above.

4. The remaining $10,000 stays in the 5.00% a/c (to the end of the month).

Explanation

1. The first $10,000 (loaned out on 4/10) earned 11 days interest at the savings bank at 5¼%, *plus* 11 days interest in the 5.00% account—to a total rate for *10* days of 11.3%. (From the 10th, the money earned something over 12% from the short-term loan.)

2. The second $10,000 (loaned out on the 11th) also earned 11 days interest at 5¼%, *plus* 12 days at 5%, to a total rate for *11* days of 10.7%.

3. The third $10,000 (loaned out on the 12th) likewise earned 11 days interest at 5¼%, *plus* 13 days at 5%, to a total rate for *12* days of 10.2%.

4. The fourth $10,000 (loan of 4/13), earned 11 days

interest at 5¼%, *plus* 14 days at 5%, to a total rate for 13 days of 9.8%.

5. The fifth $10,000 (loan of 4/14), earned 11 days interest at 5¼%, *plus* 15 days at 5%, to a total rate for 14 days of 9.5%.

6. The sixth $10,000 (loan of 4/15), earned 11 days interest at 5¼%, *plus* 16 days at 5%, to a total rate for 15 days of 9.2%.

7. The remaining (uninvested) $10,000, earned 11 days interest at 5¼%, *plus* the entire month at 5%, for a total rate for the month of 6.9%.

Conclusion

Even assuming that the short-term loans yielded the lowest rate of 12%, the total yield on $70,000 for the month of April was at the annual rate of 10.56%.

Note

A bank officer can, and usually does, clear a check deposit (waive clearance time) for a good customer, or if the depositor has cleared balances in other accounts at the bank. Otherwise, the check deposit made on the 10th would have to remain in either the 5.00% a/c or the checking a/c for four business days before a check issued against that balance would be cleared.

To the student of interest-paying practices, the 5.00% Regular Passbook Savings account's 10-day regulation presents some additional interesting opportunities on those four bonanza days—the 10th of January, April, July, and October. A deposit made on those dates and withdrawn on the:

> 20th earns 10.00% interest
> 19th earns 10.56% interest
> 18th earns 11.25% interest

17th earns 12.14% interest
16th earns 13.33% interest
15th earns 15.00% interest
14th earns 17.50% interest

And that is not all. If the account has a sufficient balance to permit withdrawals before the check deposit has cleared, or, *if cash has been deposited* on the 10th, a withdrawal on the:

13th earns 21.67% interest
12th earns 30.00% interest
11th earns 55.00% interest

Of course, percentage interest rates can be misleading, so let us examine the last figure in dollars and cents. At 5% interest, $10,000 in one day earns $1.37. At 55% interest, $10,000 in one day earns $15.07—11 times as much interest as at 5%.

It should also be understood that no bank can afford to pay interest rates of 10% to 55% as a general practice. So, whenever you discover a loophole for yourself, as you now should be able to, guard your secret jealously.

So far, you have seen that 20 days of interest can be earned in 10 days, 15 days of interest in five days, and even 11 days of interest in one day—yielding 55%. Would you believe that 11 days of interest can be earned in zero days? If you're sharp, you will know how to do it before you finish reading the following example.

Example

Assume a balance over $10,000 in the savings bank DD-DW a/c. In addition, the person either (a) has a similar balance in his 5.00% Regular Passbook Savings account; (b) has sufficient balances in other accounts at the same bank so that a check deposit for $10,000 will be cleared by an officer without having to wait four business days; or (c) is willing to carry $10,000 in cash from the savings bank in order to deposit cash into his 5.00% account.

The following accounts are needed:

#1. Savings bank DD-DW a/c (balance over $10,000)
#2. Savings bank checking a/c [not needed if (c) above is used]
#3. Chase checking a/c
#4. Chase 5.00% Regular Passbook Savings a/c (as described on page 78, or an equivalent account at another bank)

Step 1. On April 10th, write a $10,000 check on account #3 and deposit it into account #1.

Step 2A. [If (a) or (b) above is used] At the same time, transfer $10,000 from account #1 to account #2 and write a check on account #2 for $10,000. Or:

Step 2B. [If (c) above is used] At the same time, withdraw $10,000 in cash from account #1.

Note: Steps 1 and 2 leave the balance in account #1 and #3 unchanged. ($10,000 is deposited and $10,000 is withdrawn.)

Step 3. Still on the 10th, deposit the $10,000 check (from Step 2A) or $10,000 in cash (from Step 2B) into account #4.

Step 4. On the 11th (or after 3 P.M. on the 10th) transfer $10,000 from account #4 to account #3.

Explanation

Balances in the two savings bank accounts have remained unchanged. They have been used merely as a vehicle through which to "cash" the check written on account #3. At the same savings bank, no interest is gained or lost due to the transactions.

At the commercial bank, although no money was actually used, the records of the 5.00% account indicate that $10,000 was deposited on the 10th and withdrawn on the 11th. Because the bank's rules, as printed in its brochure, require that deposits through the "10th day of any quarter . . . earn interest from the first day of that quarter," interest is earned through the 11th on the $10,000 even though $10,000 is actually in the account zero days. As a matter of fact, there really is no $10,000.

And now it may occur to some readers that the interest on the mythical $10,000 could have been increased still further, provided that in the previous example Step 2A was used rather than Step 2B. The following example requires the same four accounts as previously used.

Example

Step 1. On April 10th, write a $10,000 check on account #2 and deposit it into account #4.

Step 2. On April 11th, write a $10,000 check on account #3 and deposit it into account #1. Transfer $10,000 from account #1 to account #2. (This covers check written in Step 1.)

Step 3. On April 12th, transfer $10,000 from account #4 to account #3. (This covers check written in Step 2.)

Result and Explanation

As in the previous example, balances in the two savings bank accounts remain unchanged. However, the ''mythical'' $10,000 earns interest in the 5.00% account for the first 12 days instead of the first 11.

Since Chase-Manhattan's 5.00% Regular Passbook Savings account with its own 10-day rule may be unique, perhaps it is time to return to the types of accounts available in most parts of the country.

Recall (see pages 48 and 87) that Mr. Alert had three accounts at a savings bank and two at a commercial bank as follows:

Recap

Commercial Bank	Savings Bank
1. CB/Check a/c	3. SB/Check a/c
2. CB/DD-DW a/c	4. SB/DD-DW a/c, 5¼%
	5. SB/Reg. a/c, 5¼%

Refer back to pages 88 and 89. After Steps 4 and 5, the $10,000 was in account #2 as of 4/10.

April 1978

Sun	Mon	Tue	Wed	Thu	Fri	Sat
						1
2	3	4	5	6	7	8
9	10	11	12	13	14	15
16	17	18	19	20	21	22
23	24	25	26	27	28	29
30						

Step 1. Anytime on Friday, 4/14, write a $5,000 check on account #1 and deposit it into account #4.

Step 2. After 3 P.M. on 4/14, or on Monday, 4/17,

transfer $5,000 from account #2 to account #1 (to cover check deposited in Step 1).

The result of Steps 1 and 2 is that $5,000 earns interest from both banks from the 14th through the 17th, and accounts #2 and #4 each have balances of $5,000 (plus).

It should be evident to the reader that from this point on, double interest can be earned over any weekend on the full $10,000—three to four days of double interest during any week.

Example

(From the previous example, accounts #2 and #4 each have balances slightly over $5,000.)

Step 1A. On Friday, 4/21, write two checks, each for $5,000—one on account #1 and one on account #3.

Step 1B. Deposit account #1 check into account #4 and account #3 check into account #2.

The result of Steps 1A and 1B is that balances in both account #2 and account #4 are increased by $5,000 each to $10,000 (plus) each.

Step 2. On Monday, 4/24, transfer $5,000 from account #2 to account #1 and $5,000 from account #4 to account #3. This covers checks drawn and deposited in Steps 1A and 1B.

Result

Instead of earning interest on $5,000 in each account, interest on $10,000 in each of the two accounts is earned from 4/21 to 4/24. Should the Monday after any weekend be a bank holiday, Step 2 would be accomplished on Tuesday instead of Monday, thereby increasing the double interest by one day.

In addition to earning double interest over any weekend (for three to four days), double interest can be earned on any day during the week, merely by performing Steps 1A and 1B on one day and Step 2 on the next.

Given the current availability and regulations governing checking and savings accounts, anyone can earn 10¼% (5% + 5¼%) anytime they wish. In addition, at certain times or with special accounts, significantly higher yields can be obtained on short-term investments. It has been shown, carrying the game to a *reductio ad absurdum*, that even non-existent, mythical money can earn real interest.

The several methods previously described show how the return on liquid funds can be increased for short terms. A later chapter will deal with maximizing the return on the bulk of one's estate, on monies that can be socked away for many years.

However, the methods of multiplying the return on your money described in this chapter thus far presupposes that the reader has already saved some thousands of dollars. Although the average American can build a substantial estate, all too many people have found it impossible to save a dime. For those who don't yet have several thousand dollars with which to play money games, the following pages should help you get started. And those who have managed to save a few dollars may learn that it is awfully easy to amass a fortune—*if one really wants to.*

4.

The Average Person: Mr., Mrs., or Ms.

It is not important to know that a thousand dollars invested now will grow to ten or fifteen thousand *unless you have that thousand to begin with*. Many people don't have it, and make no attempt to amass it. They live their lives from day to day, secure in the expectation that tomorrow will take care of itself. For these ostriches, loss of a job, illness, hurricane, flood, or death of the breadwinner spells catastrophe for the family. Their faces have been seen on TV news programs after every natural disaster and during every recession. Our hearts go out to these hapless victims, but only momentarily. It couldn't happen to us. But it can and does. Yet we continue to glide along, blithely oblivious to the true cost of enjoying now and not preparing for the tomorrows that inexorably arrive.

With knowledge, foresight, and determination, any average American can fare better than his neighbors. *You* can have an estate, a cushion, a nest-egg, worth hundreds of thousands of dollars!

To start, let us examine some of the statistics about that "average" American who can build a large estate, so that you can determine how close you are to that profile.

The *median* age is (approximately) 30. That means that half the people are younger than 30, half older. If the reader is younger, he or she has more time (than average) in which to build his estate. If older, he or she has less time and, therefore, possibly less opportunity to amass as much as a younger person.

There are about 73,000,000 households with an average of 2.9 persons per household, and the *average* family size is 3.4 people.

Average individual personal savings—that is, money or other financial assets plus the value of durable goods—*increases* by about $500 per year per person. (This should, but does not necessarily indicate that a family of four, for example, should be increasing its family personal savings by four times that amount per year, or $2,000.)

Individual Net Financial Worth is defined here as the value of:

1. currency and demand (checking a/c) deposits;
2. savings accounts;
3. U.S. Government and municipal securities;
4. corporate stocks and bonds;
5. insurance and pension fund reserves;
6. miscellaneous assets (including homes and the value of durable goods).

Less the total amount of:

1. mortgage debt;
2. consumer credit;
3. other liabilities.

Using this definition, the average Individual Net Financial Worth is about $7,000, from which can be extrapolated a Net Financial Worth of $28,000 for a family of four.

Note the difference in terms: the *median* age is 30; therefore, as many people are less than 30 as are older. However, the *average* Net Worth does *not* indicate that half the people are worth less than $7,000 and a half have more. It is arrived at by dividing the total *national* Net Worth by the total population.

Recently, the total of financial and durable assets was estimated at $2,183 billion, while debt and other liabilities stood at $702 billion, giving a total Financial Net Worth of $1,481 billion ($2,183 bl. — $702 bl.). This $1,481 bl. divided by the total population rendered the statistic of Individual Net Financial Worth at $7,000.

A few individuals have Net Worths in the billions or hundreds of millions. Some thousands of people are worth over a million, while hundreds of thousands, if not a few million, can count their net assets in the hundreds of thousands of dollars. How does this affect the average? More than 200 million have *less*—less than $7,000.

Suppose we look at the imaginary town of Acirema, USA, with a population of 1,000. There are 344 homes and apartments, one large factory, one school, one bank, and several stores.

The factory is worth $5,000,000. The individual owner of this factory has his home on an estate at the edge of town. The value of his home and real estate, all mortgage-free, plus his personal cash assets total another $1,000,000, to an Individual Net Financial Worth of $6,000,000.

Next come two dozen Aciremans—the banker, the doctor, store owners, and factory executives. Their total combined Net Worth is $1,000,000.

Then there are 975 remaining people in this fictitious town. They all have some assets, but they also have liabilities—mortgage, personal loan, and credit card debts. Although some of the 975 have more than others, the total combined assets are counterbalanced by total combined liabilities. The total combined (and, therefore, average individual) Net Financial Worth of these 975 people is zero.

However, in compiling national statistics, not just the 975 are taken into account. All one thousand are bunched together to arrive at the statistical figure. For this town of 1,000 souls, the total combined Net Financial Worth is $7,000,000. Divide this $7,000,000 by the total number of inhabitants, 1,000, and we get an Individual Net Financial Worth of $7,000—the same as the national average.

Although the *average* Net Worth per person in this town of 1,000 is $7,000, the top 25 people average more than $7,000, while the *average* worth of the remaining 975 people is $0. So it is in this make-believe town, and so it is in this very real country.

Even though the poorest in this country may live better than the average person elsewhere, here and now the really great wealth is owned by a very small percentage of the people; the overwhelming majority of the population average little more than nothing. Many of us are in the same boat as are the 975 inhabitants of the town of Acirema, yet, although their *average* net worth is nothing, of the 975, some have more and some have less, or, put another way, some have greater assets than liabilities while others have debts greater than their assets.

Let's examine the life styles of some of the town's inhabitants. The working population consists mainly of factory workers, civil servants, retail store clerks, and a few domestics. There is no marked difference in wage scales—the unionized factory help earn just about as much as the teachers, policemen, and junior executives. Only store clerks and menials fare less well.

Don't for a moment labor under the delusion that the 975 Aciremans are underprivileged; they are typical Americans. Most live in their own, albeit mortgaged, homes; just about everyone owns automobiles and color TV sets. All can eat well, if they so desire, dress in reasonable (if not haute couture) fashion, enjoy the plays, operas, and concerts that periodically arrive in the nearby good-sized towns. There are few, if any, dead-beats; most have, or could get, good credit ratings. Not one of the 975 has gone through bankruptcy. But their average Net Financial Worth is zero.

Half of the households have loans from the banks—home improvement, car, and personal loans—on which they make monthly payments—at 12% or more interest. And as debit balances decrease, additional loans are assumed to pay for other needed or wanted things or services.

Three quarters of the families have credit cards from Sears and other chains, oil companies, plus Master Charge and VISA, etc. Most manage to meet the monthly payments on their unpaid balances—at 12% to 18% interest.

Only one fourth have no debts at all—except for the current month's utiliities—but most of them, in typical American fashion, live from weekly paycheck to weekly paycheck.

It all boils down to the simple fact that 90% of the 975 ordinary citizens of Acirema, USA, have no real savings; 75% have debts greater than assets. Put another way, 75% have a *negative* Net Financial Worth; 15% have, roughly, a zero worth; while only 10% have a *positive* financial worth. In this town of 1,000 souls, one is "rich" and 24 are "upper middle class." The remaining 975 have basically the same earned incomes, yet 90% have nothing or less than nothing, while 10% of the 975, or less than 100 people, have nest-eggs of varying sizes. Nevertheless, a *few* of these "low income" individuals are actually worth several several hundred thousand dollars each—more than any one of the 24 "upper middle class" folks are worth.

The savings or estates of the 90-odd working people who have them were built with their own hands and minds and characters. Not one of them inherited a sou; none made a killing in the market; there were no gambling winnings since not one of them wasted precious dollars on lotteries, horses, or casinos. Their average earned income has been about the same as the average of the rest of their 975 fellow citizens. These 10% "have it made"; the remaining 90% live from hand to mouth.

How did one out of ten achieve financial success and security? In addition to earned income, each of them managed to get *unearned* income. When one works for wages, commissions, or fees, or gains income from a profession, that income is *earned*. However, when money makes more money—like earnings from investments and interest on savings—that is *unearned* income. And every one of the 90-odd people who have real Net Financial Worth in Acirema has unearned income every year. And each year's unearned income amounts to more than the previous ones.

Almost every one of the 975 Aciremans could have unearned income if he really wanted it. But only 10% did.

Almost every average American can have sizeable unearned income, but only a very small percentage do. The secret of wealth for the average person is unearned income—and it's yours practically for the asking. Let us look behind the drawn shades of Acirema into the private lives of a few of the inhabitants and see for ourselves how a few have managed to make it while the majority have not.

Living in similar houses within a block of each other are two teachers, Ned and Paul, who have worked together for 20 years at the high school in the county seat 10 miles east of Acirema. Both have been married for 18 years; neither of their wives earn any income, devoting their energies to their families, the PTA, and volunteer work at the hospital. Each of the two families has one child in the local elementary school and one in the secondary school at which Ned and Paul teach. Both their salaries are, and have been, identical. Neither family inherited wealth, neither has suffered catastrophic illness, nor has either had to pay the bills for anyone outside of his immediate family of four. The men leave for school at 7:45 A.M. and return at 3:30 P.M., traveling together and alternating the driving. Here, though, their similarities cease.

Ned enjoys driving to work. His automobile is expensive, comfortable, prestigious, and new—never more than two years old. On his car's second anniversary, his wife takes it over and Ned trades-in her four-year-old on a new model for himself. Over his years as a tenured teacher with seniority increments, he gradually traded up from the basic, stripped Ford-Plymouth-Chevy class to the full-sized, fully-equipped cars.

For Ned and his wife, their cars are a basic necessity. After all, Ned puts his life on the line every time he has to drive to work to earn his living. A big new car is safer. If his wife didn't have a car of her own, she would be a prisoner of the house every other workday. It's no fun to wait on street corners for a bus, and who would dream of walking? Two-car families are the rule, not the exception.

The thrill and prestige of driving a brand-new car far out-weighs the cost. The trade-in value of his wife's four-year-old covers the down payment on the new car. The balance is paid out in easy monthly payments for three years—at 10% to 12% interest. For the first year of new car ownership, Ned meets payments on both his new and his wife's old cars, but the second year, when only the now-not-so-new car is being paid off, Ned feels rich enough to take on other obligations.

The sense of self-importance that Ned achieves through prestige car ownership would scarcely permit him to brown-bag it to work, so he goes out for lunch to the restaurants near his school.

Living in the cultural wasteland of Acirema is not very stimulating for an educated couple like Ned and his wife. So once a year they fly off to the Big Apple for two weeks of culture, enough to sustain them through the remaining 50 weeks. It's matinee and evening performances at the Broadway theatres, the concerts, ballet, and opera. And how can one take this kind of vacation without sampling the culinary delights of the many fine (and expensive) restaurants? After all, you only live once.

For Ned, this, too, is no extravagance. It is the breath of life for one who must spend most of the year in the doldrums, enlivened only occasionally by road companies of shows and a few cultural events that appear in the nearby big town and which he and his wife attend religiously. It is this exposure to drama, music, and art that provides both man and wife with the stuff of which good social conversation is made at the country club to which they (naturally) belong. Everyone who is anyone belongs to the club—where all experiences are invariably described by one adjective: fabulous. Ned makes good use of the word since two weeks after his theatre vacations he finds it hard to remember the plots of any of the plays and cannot recall which actor played in what musical. But each show, every concert, all the operas were—fabulous. (In addition to the New York trips, there were winter recess voyages to the Caribbean and Hawaii, a trip to Europe, and a junket to Las Vegas.)

As the balance due on their 30-year, 6% mortgage slowly decreased, Ned realized that it was an absolute necessity to add a family room to their home. No one in the smart set entertained in the living room any more. Instead of a "home improvement loan" at 12%, man and wife refinanced their 6% mortgage (which would have been paid off in 13 years) with a brand new 8½% one that provided the wherewithal for the new family room. So what if it will take 12 more years before his home is free and clear?

Cows may chew grass and say moo, but educated, intelligent professionals know how to, and have the right to, live graciously. And there is nothing quite as gracious as the sipping of a fine Chablis, Pouilly-Fuisse or Mouton-Cadet nightly with dinner (for the trifling cost of $50 per case). The Moet et Chandon is reserved for special occasions.

One hardly expects the wife of a professional to clean house and prepare all the meals, so a cleaning lady comes on Thursdays and the couple eats out at least once each week while their children prepare a TV dinner—to eat while watching their new console color TV (bought, of course, on time).

We could go on to learn that the money saved on auto collision insurance every other year, plus a few dollars, goes toward the necessary periodic fur coat remodeling, but we won't. We get the picture. Ned lives the good life, enjoying much of what has been made attainable to the average American. There has been only one problem, one which has arisen during the last few years.

After the oil embargo of early '74, and the consequent gasoline price increases, Ned expected that his union would get raises for him at least large enough to compensate for the oil-induced inflation, so that he could maintain the standard of living he had become accustomed to and to which he felt he had an inalienable right. His union did prevail upon the Board of Education, but the populace, as badly hurt by the cost of living increases as the teachers, could not face or afford an inordinate jump in school taxes. The school budget was defeated. *And* defeated a *second* time by an even wider margin.

So the teachers, like almost everyone else, had to settle for increases not quite large enough to offset the increased cost of living. To any logical and realistic person, this situation indicated —demanded—a decrease in one's living standard to keep the weekly budget balanced. But not to Ned—or to millions like him. He had become used to gracious living; he was entitled to it; he would not pull in the reins on spending, particularly since his credit was good. By next year, or the year after, teachers' salaries would catch up.

Now, several years later, Ned's pay still hasn't caught up. Nor has almost anyone else's. It is a fact of life that energy now takes a far larger percentage of spendable income than it did five or ten years ago. And Ned hasn't yet made one step toward using less of that now-more-expensive energy, gasoline; his last two new-car purchases were still in the gas guzzling class.

Parenthetically, it is interesting to note that over the past 25 years the cost of most necessities—food, transportation, housing, even the daily newspaper—has risen to eight or ten times previous cost. Oddly enough, those goods and services, the prices of which we complain the most about, like electricity, the telephone and gasoline at the filling station pump, have risen the least. Electricity is double to two and a half times its price of a quarter century ago, the "5¢ phone call" is 10¢ to 20¢ and monthly charges have doubled. But most long-distance calls have come down in price. Even the much-complained-about gasoline has risen only two to three times previous cost. Compare that with the penny postcard for 11¢, the $50 apartment for $400, the 5¢ bus ride for 50¢ to 75¢, the 2¢ newspaper for 20¢, or the can of coffee, bag of sugar, and loaf of bread.

The picture of Ned's way of life may seem exaggerated and distorted, but it isn't. Most people do much the same as Ned does: they live beyond their incomes. Before they are aware of it, particularly those whose incomes seem to warrant graceful living, they are in debt so far over their heads that the rest of their lives will be devoted to working for their creditors.

Now let us take a glimpse of the life style of Ned's counterpart, Paul. From the very start, the two differed in their outlooks. Though both were born during the Great Depression and knew how their parents had suffered and struggled to keep a roof over their heads, Ned entered adult life with an unconscious but nevertheless overwhelming need to have those things that represent wealth and comfort. Clothes make the man; appearance is everything; an air of success insures success.

Paul, by comparison, craved security. While the entire country reveled in delirious prosperity, Paul started married life with the firm resolve that he would protect his fledgling family against the time when the bubble might burst, when disaster would strike through recession or depression or sickness or natural catastrophe. Umbrellas protect against rain, he thought, and savings against most personal crises.

On the other hand, Paul knew that living as a miser was not the answer. He knew he must strike a balance between getting everything he could afford, and saving everything for a rainy day. He could afford all necessities and some, but not all, luxuries—*if* he were to attain his goal of financial independence. All that would be required would be sound judgment, planning, and a little restraint.

At the time of his marriage, Paul had a two-year-old stripped-down low-priced car. He and his bride had vetoed the idea of going into hock to get a second car so both could have "wheels." Since he drove to work only on alternate days, his wife had the use of the car every other day and, when needed, after 3:30 P.M. on those days when Paul drove. Should any real emergency arise at the times she was car-less, she could always take a bus or call a cab.

Paul had read that companies pay out on collision insurance less than half of the amount collected in premiums, so he never took that $100 deductible item; instead, he put the same amount as the premium into a separate interest-bearing "collision" account, and withdrew from the account only those repair costs in excess of the $100 deductible. Now, 18 years later, because of compounded interest on the unspent balances, that account has more money in it than the total that he had put in over the years.

Paul kept his car in good shape and "running like a clock" until their 10th anniversary. He had learned that, ordinarily, the lowest cost-per-mile of automobile ownership is achieved if a car is kept for 100,000 miles, regardless of its age. All that was needed was regular preventive maintenance; and most of this, like changing oil, filters, points and plugs, he learned to do himself at whopping savings.

Lunching out was no big attraction to Paul, particularly after he calculated that restaurant-bought food, adding tax and tip to

cost, totalled about four times the price of the ingredients. So he
seldom joined Ned, preferring to bring from home his fresh
fruit, sandwich, and beverage, and joining several of his compatriots in the teachers' lounge at noon. At today's prices, his
savings on lunches came to about $350 a year (for the teachers'
180-day year).

Paul has learned not to sneeze at a $350 saving. He knows
that at today's possible interest rates $350 will grow to almost
$2,300 by the time he retires—and that $5,000 saved in the first
few years of adult life (at today's available interest rates) grows
to more than $125,000 by retirement age!

However, the teacher well knew, as the cliche goes, that man
does not live by bread alone. All saving and no spending is as
unwise as the reverse. One must have pleasures to look forward
to; anticipation is more enjoyable than realization, but retirement in luxury is too distant. So for two years Paul and his wife
dreamed of and planned for their 10th anniversary—an all-
summer trip through Europe.

In advance, they rented a small apartment outside of Paris, to
use as the focal point from which to make side trips all over the
continent. For this, they bought a new 1969 VW Squareback (a
small station wagon) to be picked up at a VW dealer in Paris. At
the end of their vacation, having covered 3,500 miles, the VW
was shipped to their home in the USA. Today, eight years later,
the car still runs like new, Paul having kept it in good shape by
doing most of the regular service himself.

Although well educated in the arts, Paul long ago became dis-
enchanted with theatre and opera. He had come to the conclusion that not more than one show in 20 he had seen had been
really worth the hassle, rush, and cost of the night out. A production that could hardly be remembered a few weeks after it
had been seen just wasn't worth blowing a day's pay on. Instead, Paul found exhilaration in reading the plays and popular
novels and listening to the operas and concerts in the comfort of

his living room. Reading and listening stimulated his imagination; the scenes he envisaged were far more exciting and satisfying than sitting passively in a theatre being entertained. These exercises in imagination were, to him, like the savoring of a good meal compared to an intravenous injection—of culture.

Almost all of the books he ever wanted to read were available at the public library, while recordings of complete operas or symphonies, which could be listened to time after time, were available at less than the cost of one ticket to the live—and often second rate—performance.

And Paul cashed in on fringe benefits available at the library. He learned how to do a better-than-professional paint job in his home, how to repair the washing machine, dryer, and TV without falling prey to the notoriously expensive and often incompetent repair services. (At present-day costs, Paul figures that $600 a year must be set aside to have the house painted inside and out every five years. By doing it himself a little at a time, the cost is less than $50 a year, with an annual saving of $550.)

Paul and his wife gravitated toward a small group of people who entertained each other weekly in alternate homes with coffee and cake and endless talk about politics, current events, philosophy, and myriad other interests. To this group, the liquor-laden, inane conversations of the pseudo-sophisticated country club crowd were a drag, so there was no compelling reason for Paul or the others to plunk down hard cash for a club bond, nor pay its annual dues and periodic assessments. Lacking a country club, theatres, and opera houses at which to show it off, Paul's wife has had no want of a fur coat and no need to have it remodeled periodically.

Two news photos and a TV commercial have had a profound effect on the well-read high school teacher. One was the picture of Adlai E. Stevenson with a hole in the sole of his shoe; the second was one of Nelson Rockefeller in patched trousers, while the commercial showed a German tycoon with a new

Volkswagon saying, "It isn't that I can't afford to own a Mercedes, it's that I can afford *not* to!" As were Stevenson, Rockefeller, and the German industrialist, Paul, too, is sufficiently secure not to require prestige clothes or cars. In addition, he has carried on his own personal war against the planned obsolescence of our technology; he is proud that he keeps his household appliances running in good condition even longer than he does his automobile. Nor is he seduced by the advertising for every newfangled fad gadget that in short order clutters the closets and attics of Acirema (and all of America, for that matter).

Though his interests and pursuits cost him little, they are every bit as enjoyable as Ned's, and of more enduring value. Paul has never had the occasion to borrow money to finance his whims. Indeed, it is *his* banked savings that are used for loans to the Neds of Acirema. Paul spends—and squanders—fewer of his hard-earned dollars than does Ned. Just on the cost of car ownership, Paul saves more than a couple thousand dollars a year! As he has spent less, he has saved more.

As his savings grew, they produced more and more *unearned income* on top of his teacher's salary. Today, that *unearned* income exceeds his *earned* income. If he so desired, Paul could quit work today and live better in retirement than can Ned by continuing at his daily grind, for Paul has no debts, but rather has built an estate, while Ned has mortgaged his future earnings, and his life, for the sake of quickly forgotten baubles and spangles.

Paul enjoys a peace of mind Ned will never know. He has no need to try to impress others with Cadillacs and Cardins, Guccis and Givenchys. He can afford not to!

Not far from where the two teachers live is a block of similar homes in which some of the employees of the town's large factory live. Their wages are similar to Ned's and Paul's. Their union, as George Meany aptly put it, has brought them from the incomes and interests of the working class to those of the middle class. All, save one, live in what has come to be known as The American Way. They enjoy much of what this good land has to offer—backyard swimming pools, hi-fi stereos, jazzy cars, daily visits to the neighborhood tavern, stylish clothing, perfumes (even for the men), sporting events, discos, and gadgets, gadgets, and more gadgets.

Their needs and desires may differ in style from Ned's, but the effect is much the same. They spend their money on virtually whatever is available. And when they make additional money, there is always something to spend it on, something they absolutely must have. After all, that's what money is for. Like Ned, many have needs and wants richer than their pocketbooks. So they, too, go into revolving debt via credit cards, long-term debt through bank loans and second mortgages, and usurious debt thanks to the good offices of the friendly finance companies.

Only one on the entire block (we'll call him Bob) ever learned Ben Franklin's axiom: "A penny saved is . . . ." He works and plays hard, eats, dresses, and generally lives well, but not extravagantly. He thinks twice before buying unneeded luxuries, almost invariably passes up his peers' invitations to the local bar, limits costly transitory pleasures, eliminates most unnecessary frills, and invests in hobbies that interest him but also gradually grow in monetary value.

And as in so many families today, his wife works—part time as a sales clerk. They live within *his* income and save something out of it each week. All of his wife's earnings go into the bank. Like Paul, Bob has built an estate that provides the family with unearned income—which is not spent, but rather left to accrue more interest. By the time they are ready to retire, Bob and Paul will be the second and third richest men in Acirema. Only the factory owner with assets of several million will be worth more. And with life expectancies increasing steadily, what could be nicer than anticipating decades of luxurious retirement, having both the time and the wherewithal to satisfy every dream, and being able to leave enough to their children to assure their comfort?

Compare these golden years with those of a widowed senior citizen on Social Security interviewed recently on the TV news. Wearing what appeared to be a 20-year-old mangy mink coat, this pitiful soul had been reduced to eating dog food because of the high cost of everything. Had the cost of that mink coat been saved rather than spent, today the interest alone would provide her with the finest of food.

Compared to the average person anywhere else in the world, the overwhelming majority of Americans have a greater opportunity to obtain all of the necessities of life, plus some of its luxuries, and *still* build a capital base. Fortunately for the Pauls and Bobs, and others who have built up some security, most people opt for too many luxuries, con themselves into believing they are necessities, then live from hand to mouth, spend everything they earn—and more. Yes, it is fortunate for Paul and Bob that the multitudes never amass any wealth.

This country runs on conspicuous, extravagant and unnecessary consumption. To keep the economy going, it has been necessary to sell, even if people haven't yet earned the money with which to buy. Therefore, easy credit. Get the people to spend. What matter if they mortgage their future earnings and face lifelong debt in order to spend today? Hence, the avalanche of credit cards . . . time payments . . . personal loans . . . mortgages.

And if that sounds idiotic, think what would happen if those who have been spending like the proverbial drunken sailor stopped. Stopped spending, started to repay debts, and then started to save!

Sales would drop—dead! A small drop in sales figures signals recession, a big drop, panic. If everyone with a net worth of less than that average $7,000 were to stop spending more than they earn, and start saving until they reached the $7,000 average figure, we'd quickly tumble into the worst depression ever experienced. Business would be bankrupt, the stock market would crash, and unemployment would reach 30% or 50%. The wheels of industry would grind to a halt.

What effect would that have on Paul and Bob? Wouldn't prices tumble so that more could be bought with their wealth? Perhaps, if—and that is a big IF—they had had the foresight to liquidate their investments—including bank accounts—before the crash and converted the bulk of their assets into hard cash and gold. How many would have had that foresight and timing? How many had it in 1929?

More likely, Paul and Bob would be in almost as bad shape as the others. First, both would be in as great a jeopardy of losing their jobs as anyone else. Second, the value of their investments would tumble—even if all of their capital were in insured bank savings. That's correct. In a crash, insured savings stand a good chance of being wiped out.

Why? Because there are only a few pennies in federal insurance funds available to cover every $100 of insured savings. This is more than sufficient to cover depositors when an occasional bank fails. But in the type of situation just hypothesized, banks all across the land would fail.

The Federal insuring agencies rely on their ability to *liquidate* the failed banks' assets, assets which are primarily in mortgages, business loans, personal loans, stocks, and bonds. But there would be few, if any, bidders for these assets, so mortgages, stocks, and bond certificates might as well be sold as paper— with which landlords could cover the walls of the thousands of magnificent new banking edifices. Few business loans would be collectible—with more companies going bankrupt than surviving. And personal loans? In this kind of depression, how many could repay credit card advances and loans? With what? Their unemployment insurance?

Of course, the Congress in its infinite wisdom could bail out the private banking system (as it did a certain aircraft manufacturer and a certain city) by authorizing the Treasury to provide the insuring agencies with something like a trillion newly-printed dollars—which would be as worthless as 1918 German Marks.

Either alternative would be disastrous. Our economy survives on buying with borrowed money. We need at least three-fourths of our population perpetually indentured to the banks. If great masses of people would not borrow to buy, business would stagnate and die. So, once again, if you want to be rich, financially independent, do it for yourself and keep it to yourself. Don't become a missionary.

In summary, for those who have resolved to achieve financial security, it is most important to realize that instant gratification brings no lasting joy; impulse buying is the enemy. Anticipation whets one's appetite—and provides the time and opportunity to recognize that many of our desires are merely passing fancies and hardly worth sacrificing security for.

Plan your purchases, expenditures, vacations, and occasional splurges long in advance. Dream about realizing them. Savor your satisfaction when you finally have what you have wanted for so long. Anticipation is more than half the fun.

"But it only costs $100." Don't buy it! Unspent, that $100 will become $1,700! As you will see.

5.

"The Highest Rate the Law Allows" Ha!

"It takes money to make money," is an old cliche. Nonsense! All it takes for the average American to obtain the money with which to make more money is desire and determination. And, once this money has been obtained, there are many games that can be played with money and banks that result in a decent amount of unearned income which can then set aside to start one's estate-building program. Bouncing funds from bank to bank can provide an additional few hundred dollars a year. In time, each of those hundreds can grow fifteen or twenty times over.

As one amasses funds, it becomes desirable that the money multiply as quickly as possible with safety, but without the necessity of switching money from place to place. The wealthier we get to be, the lazier we become; even going to the bank can become a chore.

Over any long period of time, interest rates may go upward or downward. Likewise with the income taxes one is required to pay. There are numerous "shelters"—ways to defer or completely avoid the payment of much of one's taxes, but that is not the subject of this work; it would require a volume by itself. However, once the building of an estate has been started and income increases, it would be well to study up on tax sheltering and avoidance, or seek professional guidance.

Note: All calculations and projections of earnings are gross before taxes and are based on rates that are currently offered throughout the country. Since interest rates may rise or fall, projections of interest earnings are based on current (April, 1979) rates.

Let us say that on the same day last year, four average Americans deposited $1,000 each into new savings instruments at four different banks. No withdrawals or additional deposits were or will be made; interest accrues. The first opened the account in one of the largest banks in the country; the remaining three went to banks which all advertised "the highest rates the law allows." Let us check the amount of interest each will earn.

> The first will earn $3,788.44 in interest,
> The second, $4,692.46;
> The third, $6,174.16; while
> The fourth will earn $16,101.50—or 2.6 times as much as the third, 3.4 times as much as the second and 4¼ TIMES BETTER THAN THE FIRST!

Let us examine how and why one of the four will do so much better than the other three. The answer is simple. The fourth was willing to take a tiny gamble—not with his principal, but with the amount of interest he would earn. At the time the accounts were opened, none of the four knew when or if they would need the money. All hoped that these first deposits would remain in the bank earning interest, the start of their individual estates.

Unlike the fourth, the first three played it safe; their monies went into day of deposit to day of withdrawal savings accounts. Funds could be withdrawn at any time without penalty or loss of interest.

There were no large signs proudly proclaiming it, so the first depositor was unaware that this bank, one of the "big three," paid only 4½% compounded quarterly on these accounts, giving a yield of 4.5765% (annually). He assumed the bank paid "the highest rates the law allows"—but it didn't, and he didn't ask, nor is he the type to *check* his quarterly earnings. So, at 4½%, $3,788.49 will be earned.

The second opened the account at an equally large bank that did offer "the highest rates . . . ." But the highest rate for that type of account in that type of bank was 5%, and compounding was quarterly, so the yield came to 5.0945%. The interest earned will be $4,692.46, or about $900 more than the first account!

The third took his choice of many savings banks and savings and loan associations and also received "the highest rates . . . ," which in this case was the nominal rate of 5¼% compounded daily to yield 5.47%. Interest will total $6,174.16 or almost $2400 more than the first person will earn at the giant bank—on an initial deposit of $1,000.

The fourth was a gambler. (Not *much* of a gambler, but still . . . .) He decided to put his money into an 8% savings certificate yielding 8.45%. The certificate does not mature for at least eight years, and if he has to withdraw funds prior to maturity he will be penalized. But he realized the penalty was hardly severe: Premature withdrawal required that interest be recomputed at 5¼% yielding 5.47% and that 90 days of interest be forfeited.

He chose to gamble on the eight-year higher rate for several reasons: the reward was much larger, the penalty small; he intends to continue saving more and more, so the chance of his needing the money prior to maturity of the certificate is remote and, in addition, should the unlikely eventuality arise, he could borrow against the collateral of the certificate and still come out better than with a savings account like the other three had taken.

Eight percent is 78% more than 4½%, 60% more than 5% and 52% more than 5¼%. But 8% will earn $16,101.50 while

4½% earns only $3,788.44, 5% earns $4,692.46 and 5¼%
earns $6,174.16. Therefore, 8% earns 425% (not 78%) more
than 4½%, 343% (not 60%) more than 5%, and 261% (not
52%) more than 5¼%!

Why is there this apparent inconsistency? Compare doubling
money each year with tripling it. Double $1 annually for three
years and you have $8 (2, 4, 8), with a profit of $7 (8 - 1 = 7).
Triple $1 annually for three years and you have $27 (3, 9, 27),
with a profit of $26 (27 - 1 = 26). After the first year, tripling
earns twice as much as doubling, but by the end of the third
year, earnings by tripling are almost four times as large as by
doubling. So it is with available interest rates. Over a long
period of time, even small differences in interest rates result in
great differences in earnings. (Compare 10, 20, 30 and 40-year
earnings at different rates in the tables in Chapter VI.)

As an example, if $1,000 is put into an account for a newborn
child, at age 21 the account will have grown to $2,559.27 or to
$5,493.14—depending on whether the money earned 4½%
compounded quarterly or 8% compounded continuously! In 21
years, at the lower rate, money multiplied by 2½; at the higher
rate it multiplied by 5½. Or look at it another way: $1,559.27
interest compared to $4,493.14 interest for the same period of
time!

Recall that federal statistics showed that the average person
has tangible assets of $7,000 in excess of liabilities. An average
family of 3.4 persons could have a net worth of 3.4 × $7,000 or
$23,800.

Even if only $10,000 of that $23,800 is in cash assets, without
ever saving an additional penny, that $10,000 can grow to over
$170,000 before retirement. And then, without diminishing the
estate, and in addition to Social Security and other employee
retirement funds, that estate will produce an additional income
of more than $14,450 a year—and still leave over $170,000
available for bequests to loved ones.

Not too many people have the $10,000 in cash assets. Instead, their net worths are tied up in quickly-depreciating frozen assets such as fancy cars and furs.

Now recall that the average American increases his Net Financial Worth by $500 per year. Applying reasonable thrift, for the average family that increase *could* come to $1,700. If the family *saves* $1,000 of the $1,700 instead of sinking it all into "things" that depreciate with time, that thousand per year adds an additional $206,000 to the estate, for a grand total of $375,000! An estate of this magnitude produces retirement income of almost $31,700 annually without diminishing the principal!

And don't make excuses to yourself that it can't be done; the U.S. Government statistics don't lie. The average person *has* a Net Worth of $7,000 and *does* increase his Net Worth by $500 per year.

If *you* do not have it, take stock of yourself and how you spend your money. Wouldn't you be better off if you used a little mature judgment and restraint? You can bet your mink-lined booties that you would. Stop buying hula hoops and the Emperor's New Clothes—and all the rest of the worthless junk that eats away your chance of amassing wealth. Of course, you could become rich the easy way. You might win the million dollar lottery or make a killing at the gaming tables, but

DON'T BANK ON IT!

And don't go overboard either. Saving all that you earn and not spending at all is just as unwise as squandering everything. As we are advised to eat and drink, so too, save with moderation. Oddly enough, being careful with nickels and dimes and quarters is just as, if not more, important than using caution in buying big-ticket items. Not only does the small change quickly add up to hundreds of dollars annually, but it also teaches us how to get our money's worth. An old truism states: Be careful with the pennies and the dollars will take care of themselves.

Start playing the money game; it can be more fun and is certainly more profitable than playing Monopoly. And as the dollars mount, sock them away into the highest yielding, longest-term savings instruments available at the time.

Here are a few items to think about:

> Every $100 you save *now* will give you $8 to spend *every year* for the rest of your life.

> Every $100 you save *now*, if left to grow, can become $1,700 in the nest for your eggs.

> From now on, save $1,000 a year for the next 10 years (total = $10,000) and it will become $121,962.

> Or save $1,000 a year for the next 15 years for $154,479.

> Or for 20 years for $176,153.

Immediately following are fifteen 40-year interest tables that show how a single deposit of money grows at the different rates given by banks.

And there are four tables which show how money systematically saved for 10 or more years grows when deposited at the highest currently available interest rates (8% compounded daily to yield 8.45%)—and four additional tables with which to compare long-term earnings at 7¾% (yielding 8.17%).

Look at the tables, study them, choose your goal. You, too, may decide that it is better to earn before spending rather than to spend before earning, and that perhaps security is more desirable than that new LED watch or Cuisinart Food-Processor.

6.

Interest Tables

TABLE I

YIELD WHEN COMPOUNDED

Nominal Rate		Annually	Quarterly	Daily	Continuously
5 %	(5.00)	5.00%	5.09%	5.13%	5.20%
5¼	(5.25)	5.25	5.35	5.39	5.47
5½	(5.50)	5.50	5.61	5.65	5.73
5¾	(5.75)	5.75	5.88	5.92	6.00
6	(6.00)	6.00	6.14	6.18	6.27
6½	(6.50)	6.50	6.66	6.72	6.81
6¾	(6.75)	6.75	6.92	6.98	7.08
7	(7.00)	7.00	7.19	7.25	7.35
7¼	(7.25)	7.25	7.45	7.52	7.63
7½	(7.50)	7.50	7.71	7.79	7.90
7¾	(7.75)	7.75	7.98	8.06	8.17
8	(8.00)	8.00	8.24	8.33	8.45

Table I: Yield—Effective Annual Rates for available nominal interest rates when compounded annually, quarterly, daily, and continuously.

The following tables (II-A and II-B) give the size your estate will be if you save $1,000 a year for the next 10, 15, 20, and 40 years.

The "average" American, at age 30, has 35 years in which to build an estate for retirement at age 65. The size of this estate is found next to "End of Year-35." At age 25, see "End of Year-40." At age 35, see "End of Year-30."

"Individual Retirement Accounts" (IRAs) and "Keogh" Retirement Plans for the Self-Employed can be used to build income-tax-deferred estates.

Note: The tables assume savings of $1,000 per year for 10 to 40 years. If you save $1,500, multiply the figures by 1.5; if you save $2,000, double the amounts shown.

Warning: Many banks and savings and loan associations compound interest daily rather than continuously. Table I shows the slightly higher yield obtained through continuous compounding. On short-term savings and small amounts, this difference is inconsequential. However, with long-term savings for estate-building, the small benefit of continuous compounding makes a tremendous difference—as is shown in Tables III-B through III-H.

TABLE II-A
7¾% Certificate (Yield = 8.17%)
Growth of an estate when $1,000 per year is invested for:

End of Year	10 Years	15 Years	20 Years	40 Years
1	$ 1,081.70	$ 1,081.70	$ 1,081.70	$ 1,081.70
2	2,251.77	2,251.77	2,251.77	2,251.77
3	3,517.44	3,517.44	3,517.44	3,517.44
4	4,886.51	4,886.51	4,886.51	4,886.51
5	6,367.44	6,367.44	6,367.44	6,367.44
6	7,969.36	7,969.36	7,969.36	7,969.36
7	9,702.16	9,702.16	9,702.16	9,702.16
8	11,576.53	11,576.53	11,576.53	11,576.53
9	13,604.03	13,604.03	13,604.03	13,604.03
10	15,797.18	15,797.18	15,797.18	15,797.18
11	17,087.81	18,169.51	18,169.51	18,169.51
12	18,483.88	20,735.66	20,735.66	20,735.66
13	19,994.01	23,511.46	23,511.46	23,511.46
14	21,627.52	26,514.05	26,514.05	26,514.05
15	23,394.49	29,761.95	29,761.95	29,761.95
16	25,305.82	32,193.50	33,275.20	33,275.20
17	27,373.31	34,823.71	37,075.48	37,075.48
18	29,609.71	37,668.81	41,186.25	41,186.25
19	32,028.82	40,746.35	45,632.87	45,632.87
20	34,645.57	44,075.33	50,442.78	50,442.78
21	37,476.11	47,676.28	54,563.96	55,645.66
22	40,537.91	51,571.43	59,021.84	61,273.61
23	43,849.86	55,784.82	63,843.92	67,361.36
24	47,432.39	60,342.44	69,059.97	73,946.48
25	51,307.62	65,272.42	74,702.17	81,069.61
26	55,499.45	70,605.18	80,805.34	88,774.70
27	60,033.76	76,373.62	87,407.14	97,109.29
28	64,938.52	82,613.34	94,548.30	106,124.81
29	70,244.00	89,362.85	102,272.89	115,876.90
30	75,982.93	96,663.79	110,628.58	126,425.74
31	82,190.74	104,561.22	119,666.93	137,836.42
32	88,905.72	113,103.87	129,443.71	150,179.35
33	96,169.32	122,344.45	140,019.26	163,530.70
34	104,026.35	132,339.99	151,458.83	177,972.85
35	112,525.30	143,152.16	163,833.01	193,594.93
36	121,718.61	154,847.69	177,218.16	210,493.33
37	131,663.02	167,498.74	191,696.88	228,772.33
38	142,419.88	181,183.38	207,358.51	248,544.72
39	154,055.58	195,986.06	224,299.70	269,932.52
40	166,641.92	211,998.12	242,624.98	293,067.70

Table II-A: Earnings on savings of $1,000 per year at 7¾% (Yield = 8.17%) for 10, 15, 20, and 40 years.

TABLE II-B

8% Certificate (Yield = 8.45%)

Growth of an estate when $1,000 per year is invested for:

End of Year	10 Years	15 Years	20 Years	40 Years
1	$ 1,084.50	$ 1,084.50	$ 1,084.50	$ 1,084.50
2	2,260.64	2,260.64	2,260.64	2,260.64
3	3,536.16	3,536.16	3,536.16	3,536.16
4	4,919.47	4,919.47	4,919.47	4,919.47
5	6,419.67	6,419.67	6,419.67	6,419.67
6	8,046.63	8,046.63	8,046.63	8,046.63
7	9,811.07	9,811.07	9,811.07	9,811.07
8	11,724.60	11,724.60	11,724.60	11,724.60
9	13,799.83	13,799.83	13,799.83	13,799.83
10	16,050.41	16,050.41	16,050.41	16,050.41
11	17,406.67	18,491.17	18,491.17	18,491.17
12	18,877.53	21,138.18	21,138.18	21,138.18
13	20,472.68	24,008.85	24,008.85	24,008.85
14	22,202.62	27,122.10	27,122.10	27,122.10
15	24,078.75	30,498.42	30,498.42	30,498.42
16	26,113.40	33,075.54	34,160.03	34,160.03
17	28,319.98	35,870.42	38,131.05	38,131.05
18	30,713.02	38,901.47	42,437.63	42,437.63
19	33,308.27	42,188.64	47,108.11	47,108.11
20	36,122.82	45,753.58	52,173.24	52,173.24
21	39,175.19	49,619.76	56,581.88	57,666.38
22	42,485.50	53,812.63	61,363.05	63,623.69
23	46,075.52	58,359.80	66,548.22	70,084.39
24	49,968.90	63,291.20	72,171.55	77,091.02
25	54,191.27	68,639.30	78,270.04	84,689.71
26	58,770.44	74,439.32	84,883.86	92,930.49
27	63,736.54	80,729.45	92,056.55	101,867.61
28	69,122.27	87,551.08	99,835.32	111,559.92
29	74,963.11	94,949.15	108,271.40	122,071.23
30	81,297.49	102,972.35	117,420.33	133,470.74
31	88,167.12	111,673.51	127,342.34	145,833.51
32	95,617.25	121,109.92	138,102.76	159,240.94
33	103,696.90	131,343.70	149,772.44	173,781.29
34	112,459.28	142,442.24	162,428.21	189,550.30
35	121,962.08	154,478.60	176,153.38	206,651.80
36	132,267.87	167,532.04	191,038.35	225,198.37
37	143,444.50	181,688.49	207,181.09	245,312.13
38	155,565.56	197,041.16	224,687.89	267,125.50
39	168,710.84	213,691.13	243,674.01	290,782.10
40	182,966.90	231,748.03	264,264.46	316,437.68

Table II-B: Earnings on savings of $1,000 per year at 8% (Yield = 8.45%) for 10, 15, 20, and 40 years.

Each $1,000 saved *now* can grow to more than $25,000. With $10,000 you can have from $59,891 to $256,555—depending on where, when, and how you invest it. Compare the bottom lines of Tables III-A and III-H.

The following tables show how much $10,000 will grow to if kept for as long as 40 years. (For growth of $5,000, divide the figures in the Tables by two; for $1,000, divide by 10, etc.)

The "average" American (age 30) has 35 years before retirement at age 65. To find how much $10,000 will grow to in 35 years, look at amounts next to "End of Year-35."

Compare growth at the different interest rates—4½% to 8%. You will be surprised at the difference, and should be convinced to put your "nest-egg" to work at the highest rates available.

Note: At age 25, present savings of $10,000 combined with a $1,000-a-year retirement plan produces an estate of over $570,000 ($256,555.81 + $316,437.68)!

TABLE III-A
$10,000 Deposited at:

End of Year	4½% Compounded Quarterly (Yield = 4.5765%)	5% Compounded Quarterly (Yield = 5.0945%)
1	$10,457.65	$10,509.45
2	10,936.24	11,044.85
3	11,436.74	11,607.53
4	11,960.14	12,198.88
5	12,507.50	12,820.35
6	13,079.91	13,473.48
7	13,678.51	14,159.89
8	14,304.51	14,881.27
9	14,959.16	15,639.40
10	15,643.77	16,436.15
11	16,359.71	17,273.49
12	17,108.41	18,153.49
13	17,891.38	19,078.32
14	18,710.18	20,050.27
15	19,566.45	21,071.73
16	20,461.91	22,145.23
17	21,398.35	23,273.42
18	22,377.65	24,459.08
19	23,401.76	25,705.15
20	24,472.74	27,014.70
21	25,592.73	28,390.96
22	26,763.98	29,837.34
23	27,988.83	31,357.40
24	29,269.74	32,954.90
25	30,609.27	34,633.79
26	32,010.10	36,398.21
27	33,475.04	38,252.52
28	35,007.03	40,201.29
29	36,609.13	42,249.34
30	38,284.55	44,401.73
31	40,036.64	46,663.78
32	41,868.92	49,041.07
33	43,785.05	51,539.47
34	45,788.87	54,165.15
35	47,884.40	56,924.59
36	50,075.83	59,824.61
37	52,367.55	62,872.37
38	54,764.15	66,075.40
39	57,270.43	69,441.61
40	59,891.41	72,979.31

Table III-A: Compound earnings with regular and day of deposit to day of withdrawal savings accounts at most commercial banks.
Amount $10,000 will grow to for periods up to 40 years. (Compare with Tables for term certificate rates of 7¾% to 8%.)

TABLE III-B

$10,000 Deposited at 5¼%:

End of Year	Compounded Daily (Yield = 5.39%)	Compounded Continuously (Yield = 5.47%)
1	$10,539.00	$10,547.00
2	11,107.05	11,123.92
3	11,705.72	11,732.40
4	12,336.66	12,374.16
5	13,001.61	13,051.03
6	13,702.40	13,764.92
7	14,440.96	14,517.86
8	15,219.33	15,311.99
9	16,039.65	16,149.56
10	16,904.19	17,032.94
11	17,815.33	17,964.64
12	18,775.58	18,947.31
13	19,787.58	19,983.73
14	20,854.13	21,076.84
15	21,978.17	22,229.74
16	23,162.79	23,445.71
17	24,411.26	24,728.19
18	25,727.03	26,080.82
19	27,113.72	27,507.44
20	28,575.15	29,012.10
21	30,115.35	30,599.06
22	31,738.57	32,272.83
23	33,449.28	34,038.15
24	35,252.20	35,900.04
25	37,152.29	37,863.77
26	39,154.80	39,934.92
27	41,265.24	42,119.36
28	43,489.44	44,423.29
29	45,833.52	46,853.24
30	48,303.95	49,416.11
31	50,907.53	52,119.17
32	53,651.45	54,970.09
33	56,543.26	57,976.95
34	59,590.94	61,148.29
35	62,802.89	64,493.10
36	66,187.97	68,020.87
37	69,755.50	71,741.61
38	73,515.32	75,665.88
39	77,477.80	79,804.80
40	81,653.85	84,170.12

Table III-B: Compound earnings with regular and day of deposit to day of withdrawal savings accounts at most savings banks and savings and loan associations.

5¼% compounded: (1) Daily to yield 5.39%; (2) Continuously to yield 5.47%.

TABLE III-C
$10,000 Deposited at 5¾%:

End of Year	Compounded Daily (Yield = 5.92%)	Compounded Continuously (Yield = 6.00%)
1	$10,592.00	$ 10,600.00
2	11,219.05	11,236.00
3	11,883.22	11,910.16
4	12,586.71	12,624.77
5	13,331.84	13,382.26
6	14,121.08	14,185.20
7	14,957.05	15,036.31
8	15,842.51	15,938.49
9	16,780.39	16,894.80
10	17,773.79	17,908.49
11	18,826.00	18,983.00
12	19,940.50	20,121.98
13	21,120.98	21,329.30
14	22,371.34	22,609.06
15	23,695.72	23,965.60
16	25,098.51	25,403.54
17	26,584.34	26,927.75
18	28,158.13	28,543.42
19	29,825.09	30,256.03
20	31,590.74	32,071.39
21	33,460.91	33,995.67
22	35,441.80	36,035.41
23	37,539.95	38,197.53
24	39,762.32	40,489.38
25	42,116.25	42,918.74
26	44,609.53	45,493.86
27	47,250.41	48,223.49
28	50,047.63	51,116.90
29	53,010.45	54,183.91
30	56,148.67	57,434.94
31	59,472.67	60,881.04
32	62,993.45	64,533.90
33	66,722.66	68,405.93
34	70,672.64	72,510.29
35	74,856.46	76,806.91
36	79,287.96	81,472.56
37	83,981.81	86,360.91
38	88,953.53	91,542.56
39	94,219.58	97,035.11
40	99,797.38	102,857.21

Table III-C: 5¾% Compounded: (1) Daily to yield 5.92%; (2) Continuously to yield 6.00%.

TABLE III-D

$10,000 Deposited at 6½%:

End of Year	Compounded Daily (Yield = 6.72%)	Compounded Continuously (Yield = 6.81%)
1	$ 10,672.00	$ 10,681.00
2	11,389.16	11,408.38
3	12,154.51	12,185.29
4	12,971.29	13,015.11
5	13,842.96	13,901.44
6	14,773.21	14,848.13
7	15,765.97	15,859.29
8	16,825.44	16,939.31
9	17,956.11	18,092.88
10	19,162.76	19,325.01
11	20,450.50	20,641.04
12	21,824.77	22,046.69
13	23,291.39	23,548.07
14	24,856.57	25,151.69
15	26,526.93	26,864.52
16	28,309.54	28,693.99
17	30,211.94	30,648.05
18	32,242.18	32,735.18
19	34,408.85	34,964.45
20	36,721.12	37,345.53
21	39,188.78	39,888.76
22	41,822.27	42,605.18
23	44,632,73	45,506.59
24	47,632.05	48,605.59
25	50,832.92	51,915.63
26	54,248.89	55,451.08
27	57,894.42	59,227.30
28	61,784.93	63,260.68
29	65,936.88	67,568.73
30	70,367.84	72,170.16
31	75,096.56	77,084.95
32	80,143.05	82,334.44
33	85,528.66	87,941.42
34	91,276.19	93,930.23
35	97,409.95	100,326.87
36	103,955.89	107,159.12
37	110,941.72	114,456.65
38	118,397.00	122,251.14
39	126,353.27	130,576.44
40	134,844.20	139,468.69

Table III-D: 6½% Compounded: (1) Daily to yield 6.72%; (2) Continuously to yield 6.81%.

TABLE III-E
$10,000 Deposited at 6¾ %:

End of Year	Compounded Daily (Yield = 6.98%)	Compounded Continuously (Yield = 7.08%)
1	$ 10,698.00	$ 10,708.00
2	11,444.72	11,466.13
3	12,243.56	12,277.93
4	13,098.16	13,147.21
5	14,012.41	14,078.03
6	14,990.48	15,074.75
7	16,036.82	16,142.04
8	17,156.19	17,284.90
9	18,353.69	18,508.67
10	19,634.78	19,819.08
11	21,005.29	21,222.27
12	22,471.46	22,724.81
13	24,039.97	24,333.73
14	25,717.96	26,056.56
15	27,513.07	27,901.36
16	29,433.48	29,876.78
17	31,487.94	31,992.06
18	33,685.80	34,257.10
19	36,037.07	36,682.50
20	38,552.46	39,279.62
21	41,243.42	42,060.62
22	44,122.21	45,038.51
23	47,201.94	48,227.24
24	50,496.64	51,641.73
25	54,021.31	55,297.96
26	57,792.00	59,213.06
27	61,825.88	63,405.34
28	66,141.33	67,894.44
29	70,757.99	72,701.37
30	75,696.90	77,848.63
31	80,980.54	83,360.31
32	86,632.98	89,262.22
33	92,679.96	95,581.99
34	99,149.02	102,349.19
35	106,069.62	109,595.51
36	113,473.27	117,354.87
37	121,393.70	125,663.59
38	129,866.98	134,560.57
39	138,931.69	144,087.45
40	148,629.12	154,288.84

Table III-E: 6¾ % Compounded: (1) Daily to yield 6.98%; (2) Continuously to yield 7.08%.

TABLE III-F

$10,000 Deposited at 7½%:

End of Year	Compounded Daily (Yield = 7.79%)	Compounded Continuously (Yield = 7.90%)
1	$ 10,779.00	$ 10,790.00
2	11,618.68	11,642.41
3	12,523.78	12,562.16
4	13,499.38	13,554.57
5	14,550.98	14,625.38
6	15,684.50	15,780.79
7	16,906.32	17,027.47
8	18,223.32	18,372.64
9	19,642.92	19,824.08
10	21,173.10	21,390.18
11	22,822.48	23,080.00
12	24,600.35	24,903.32
13	26,516.72	26,870.68
14	28,582.37	28,993.46
15	30,808.94	31,283.94
16	33,208.96	33,755.37
17	35,795.94	36,422.04
18	38,854.44	39,299.38
19	41,590.17	42,404.03
20	44,830.04	45,753.95
21	48,322.30	49,368.51
22	52,086.61	53,268.62
23	56,144.16	57,476.84
24	60,517.79	62,017.51
25	65,232.13	66,916.89
26	70,313.71	72,203.32
27	75,791.15	77,907.38
28	81,695.28	84,062.06
29	88,059.34	90,702.96
30	94,919.16	97,868.49
31	102,313.36	105,600.10
32	110,283.57	113,942.50
33	118,874.66	122,943.95
34	128,134.99	132,656.52
35	138,116.70	143,136.38
36	148,875.99	154,444.15
37	160,473.42	166,645.23
38	172,974.29	179,810.20
39	186,448.98	194,015.20
40	200,973.35	209.342.40

Table III-F: 7½% Compounded: (1) Daily to yield 7.79%; (2) Continuously to yield 7.90%.

TABLE III-G
$10,000 Deposited at 7¾%:

End of Year	Compounded Daily (Yield = 8.06%)	Compounded Continuously (Yield = 8.17%)
1	$ 10,806.00	$ 10,817.00
2	11,676.96	11,700.75
3	12,618.12	12,656.70
4	13,635.14	13,690.75
5	14,734.13	14,809.28
6	15,921.70	16,019.20
7	17,204.99	17,327.97
8	18,591.71	18,743.67
9	20,090.20	20,275.03
10	21,709.47	21,931.50
11	23,459.25	23,723.30
12	25,350.07	25,661.49
13	27,393.29	27,758.03
14	29,601.19	30,025.86
15	31,987.05	32,478.97
16	34,565.21	35,132.50
17	37,351.17	38,002.83
18	40,361.67	41,107.66
19	43,614.82	44,466.16
20	47,130.17	48,099.05
21	50,928.86	52,028.74
22	55,033.73	56,279.49
23	59,469.45	60,877.52
24	64,262.69	65,851.21
25	69,442.26	71,231.25
26	75,039.31	77,050.84
27	81,087.48	83,345.89
28	87,623.13	90,155.25
29	94,685.55	97,520.93
30	102,317.20	105,488.38
31	110,563.96	114,106.78
32	119,475.41	123,429.30
33	129,105.12	133,513.47
34	139,510.99	144,421.52
35	150,755.57	156,220.75
36	162,906.46	168,983.98
37	176,036.72	182,789.97
38	190,225.27	197,723.91
39	205,557.42	213,877.95
40	222,125.34	231,351.77

Table III-G: 7¾% Compounded: (1) Daily to yield 8.06%; (2) Continuously to yield 8.17%.

TABLE III-H
$10,000 Deposited at 8%:

End of Year	Compounded Daily (Yield = 8.33%)	Compounded Continuously (Yield = 8.45%)
1	$ 10,833.00	$ 10,845.00
2	11,735.39	11,761.40
3	12,712.95	12,755.24
4	13,771.93	13,833.06
5	14,919.14	15,001.95
6	16,161.90	16,269.61
7	17,508.18	17,644.40
8	18,966.62	19,135.35
9	20,546.53	20,752.28
10	22,258.06	22,505.85
11	24,112.16	24,407.59
12	26,120.70	26,470.04
13	28,296.55	28,706.75
14	30,653.65	31,132.47
15	33,207.10	33,763.17
16	35,973.25	36,616.15
17	38,969.83	39,710.22
18	42,216.01	43,065.73
19	45,732.61	46,704.78
20	49,542.13	50,651.34
21	53,668.99	54,931.37
22	58,139.62	59,573.08
23	62,982.64	64,607.00
24	68,229.10	70,066.29
25	73,912.58	75,986.89
26	80,069.50	82,407.78
27	86,739.29	89,371.24
28	93,964.67	96,923.11
29	101,791.92	105,113.11
30	110,271.18	113,995.16
31	119,456.76	123,627.75
32	129,407.50	134,074.29
33	140,187.14	145,403.56
34	151,864.72	157,690.16
35	164,515.05	171,014.97
36	178,219.15	185,465.73
37	193,064.80	201,137.58
38	209,147.09	218,133.70
39	226,569.04	236,565.99
40	245,442.24	256,555.81

Table III-H: 8% Compounded: (1) Daily to yield 8.33%; (2) Continuously to yield 8.45%.

7.

*Making Money
—With Your Credit Cards*

Perhaps unfortunately, credit cards have become a necessity. It is almost impossible to rent a car—or even buy gasoline at night—without them. They make it possible to make purchases without risking the loss of cash, but fiendishly lure too many into unneeded expenditures and unmanageable debt. The following section applies primarily to those of us who buy anything from art supplies to zircons and pay for them in cash or by check.

In addition to the obvious uses of a credit card (buy now—pay later, free short-term credit, single monthly billing for purchases), the plastic card can be used to *earn* interest—on money that has already been spent.

For this example, let's take the hypothetical case of a family with a sufficient income so that an average of $150 per week, or *$7,500 per year, can be used for purchases that are chargeable to a bank credit card. Assume that the $150 per week previously used for cash purchases had been kept as cash or else put into a checking account. In either case, no interest had been earned.

---

*In practice, some weeks will total less than $150, some more, up to the individual's credit limit on each card, big ticket items can be charged—such as part of the price of a new car, gas and repairs, clothing, etc.

But now, with the credit card, $150 per week of their total expenses will be charged, instead of being paid for in cash or by check. So, on Friday, October 4, $150 can be deposited in a daily interest account, either at a commercial bank at 5% or at an S & L or savings bank that offers 5¼% with daily interest. By Friday, the 11th, this $150 will have been spent, but now by credit card charge rather than by out-of-pocket cash. The balance in the bank account is still $150, and $150 is owed on the charge. But the balance earns interest, while the charge costs the family nothing!

Again on the following Friday, October 11, $150 of the weekly paycheck is deposited in the same account, bringing the new balance to $300. And by the 18th they owe $300. Each week another $150 is deposited, and each week the family owes an additional $150.

Remember, you get one monthly bill for everything . . . no service charge for purchases if you pay in full within 25 days of your *billing* date. Let's assume a billing date of the first of each month. By the 25th of November, the daily interest savings account will have grown to $1200, and the *billed* charges to a maximum of $600. On November 25th, and each 25th thereafter, the charges on the credit card statement, which will average about $600, should be paid from funds in the daily interest account. In that way, neither interest charges nor service charges are incurred. The $600 each month has been "borrowed" interest free until the 25th of the following month. (See Table, page 143: Use of Daily Interest Account in Conjunction With Credit Card.)

Is it worth the bother? Most people would agree that credit cards which offer one statement and one payment each month are far more convenient than paying for each purchase by cash or check. And most of us visit some bank once a week to cash or deposit the paycheck, so it is hardly an additional bother to deposit $150 per week more.

TABLE V

Use of Daily Interest Account in Conjunction With Credit Card

Daily Interest Savings Account				Credit Card Account		
Date	Deposit	Withdrawal to pay credit card Bill	Balance*	Charges credit card for previous week	Credit card bill payment	Amount owed on credit card (balance)	
10/4	$150		$ 150				
10/11	150		300	$150		$ 150	
10/18	150		450	150		150	
10/25	150		450	150		450	
11/1	150		750	150		600	A
11/8	150		900	150		750	
11/15	150		1,050	150		900	
11/22	150		1,200	150		1,050	
11/25		$600	600		$600	450	A
11/29	150		750	150		600	B
12/6	150		900	150		750	
12/13	150		1,050	150		900	
12/20	150		1,200	150		1,050	
12/26		600	600		600	450	B
12/27	150		750	150		600	C
1/3	150		900	150		750	
1/10	150		1,050	150		900	
1/17	150		1,200	150		1,050	
1/24	150		1,350	150		1,200	
1/24		600	750		600	600	C
1/31	150		900	150		750	D
2/7	150		1,050	150		900	
2/14	150		1,200	150		1,050	
2/21	150		1,350	150		1,200	
2/25		750	600		750	450	D
2/28	150		750	150		600	

A: Credit Card bill dated 11/1, due 11/26
B: Credit Card bill dated 12/1, due 12/26
C: Credit Card bill dated 1/1, due 1/26
D: Credit Card bill dated 2/1, due 2/26

---

*Average balance for one year is more than $950, which earns approximately 50 interest.

And one asks, as all are prone to do these days, "What's in it for me?" After the first month, you'll earn about $50 per year. Not a great deal, but it's free, and will still pay for a good pair of shoes or a night on the town for you and your wife. And if your charges exceed $150 per week, proportionately more will be earned as daily interest.

This explanation of the use of a bank credit card was included not just to show the way to earn a few dollars. It demonstrates that banks are anxious to lend money without any charge whatsoever, provided circumstances are such that by so doing, the banks, too, earn money. For many years now, the credit card companies have demonstrated that, under certain circumstances, personal credit need not be usurious to be profitable. In fact, it has been proven profitable when credit is given free of interest.

It appears that we really get something for nothing, but what is it that's said about appearances? Why should any organization be anxious to extend credit and risk without charging the beneficiary?

Just as business yields to labor and then passes the charge along to the public, so credit card plans give free credit (for a limited time) to cardholders because a third party, the merchant, pays the bill, and then some.

Credit card plans charge the merchant up to 7% of the total sale. Many merchants have complained that the card companies do not pay them until 90 to 120 days after the sale of merchandise; bank charge plans charge the merchant less than the prestige card companies and pay the vendors much sooner, even immediately. As long as the cardholder pays the bank plan by the 25th of the month following the statement, the bank plan earns a commission or service charge totaling as much as 5% of the gross sale—including sales tax. But if the cardholder doesn't pay in full by the 25th, the bank collects from the cardholder (in most states) 1½% per month on the unpaid balance that doesn't exceed $500 and 1% per month on the portion that exceeds $500. These are equivalent to annual interest rates of approximately 18% and 12%—compounded monthly!

For the bank plan, the economics are simple and impressive. If the bank lays out no money after the 25th of the month, it makes as much as 5% for 25 days. And that is not per year. It represents an interest rate of about 70% a year. Actually it is a commission or service charge. And if the bank does lend out money, by paying the merchant even though the cardholder has not paid by the 25th, it collects the initial percentage *plus* over 18% per annum on sums up to $500, and over 12% on the part that exceeds $500.

As opposed to the banks that issue credit cards, the major credit card companies have not charged interest if a bill is paid late. All that they do at most is limit or cut off credit. Not having to pay 1½% per month interest, many cardholders have not been compulsive about making prompt payment, so the card company waited longer, up to 60 days longer, but the credit card companies charge an annual fee for the use of *their* cards.

Now, back to the family that spent $150 per month via a bank credit card plan and paid the bills on the 25th of the month following each statement. If they spent $20 a year for one of the major credit cards and were able to delay paying the monthly bill until two months after the 25th, they would come out ahead as compared to a bank charge card, because the balance in their daily interest account would have been *increased* by over $1200, which yields an additional $65 in interest for a year—to a total of about $115. However, there are fewer opportunities to use the prestige cards. Bank cards boast over a million merchants who honor their cards while American Express, Diners Club, etc., seem to cater to the more prestigious vendors.

To sum up: Through the use of bank credit cards, daily interest can be earned for an average of 40 days after the purchases are made. This is interest on money already spent, and the yield is infinite, since it is earnings on nonexistent funds.

And when the bank-issued credit card system is analyzed, the huge bank profits and the merchants' costs are all paid for in full by you, the consumer, to the tune of an additional price increase of about 7%—7% added on top of continuously inflating prices.

Why?

Consider an item that the merchant must sell for $1.00 to cover costs and profit. To receive this $1.00 on a credit card sale, he must charge $1.07, the 7 cents being the approximate credit card service charge and charge machine costs.

As greater numbers of customers use credit cards, prices are forced upward by 7%. As people pay 7% more for goods and services, they, too, must look to increase their spendable funds by 7%. To accomplish this end, both labor and the businessman seek to increase their return through higher wages and prices. And the merchants trapped by the credit cards, being consumers themselves, must now raise their prices again—over and above the 7% increase—to increase their own personal spendable funds.

The credit card, in all its forms, creates a strong inflationary pressure.

The consumer can attempt to combat this pressure by refusing to use credit cards, buying only for cash, and *insisting* on receiving a 5% or 6% discount for cash at any establishment that honors credit cards. Remember, the merchant must pay the credit card issuer charges as high as 7%. As a cash customer, you are entitled to this discount, since cash less 5% nets to the merchant about the same amount as does a full-price credit-card sale.

What masquerades as interest-free credit is really credit at about 70% per year—6% per month.

The blanketing of the country with bank-issued credit cards points up a system whereby the cost of consumer credit is borne by the entire consuming population rather than by those who make use of the credit. Let the borrower pay for credit, not the merchant who thereby forces the cash customer, the general public, to foot the bill. Price-fixed goods or services such as airline tickets are most unconscionable examples of the public being forced to underwrite credit costs. A vendor such as an airline is not permitted by law or regulation to extend a cash discount.

8.

Tax-Sheltered Pension Plans—Advantages And Disadvantages

There are many reasons for saving: to buy such expensive items as a home or automobile, to create an umbrella for that rainy day of illness or unemployment, to provide for income in retirement, and to ease the burdens of loved ones, either while we live or after we are gone. These savings, however, quickly become almost worthless when inflation reduces the buying power of the dollars saved. It is therefore important to see to it that the dollars thus set aside grow at a sufficiently high rate to offset the effects of inflation. Thus, when the inflation rate is, for example, 10%, our savings must grow by 10% *just to maintain their value.*

But both federal and state governments claim that this growth—which isn't growth at all—is income and therefore subject to income taxes. Consequently, if inflation is running at a rate of 10%, savings must grow on the average by 15%, because income taxes will take away a third or more of that 15%, leaving the saver with a net of 10%—which is just enough to offset inflation's erosion of the dollar's value.

It isn't easy to make savings grow by 15% or more. An alternative is to avoid income taxes on savings "growth" or interest.

One way to avoid these taxes is to buy such tax-exempt instruments as municipal bonds. But such bonds, because interest is exempt from income taxes, generally pay much lower rates than taxable instruments; municipal bonds may therefore be excellent investments for those in the 50% or higher brackets, but they make no sense for the average family.

Another way to avoid taxes on interest or dividends is through government-approved retirement plans. Of even greater importance and benefit to the taxpayer is the fact that income that is put into a retirement plan is also free of current income taxes.

Prior to 1967, only employees of larger companies and governmental organizations enjoyed the tax benefits of retirement plans. Thus, as an example, a policeman in the greater metropolitan New York area who now earns $23,000 a year, pays income taxes on that $23,000, less his deductions and exemptions. His employer, the municipality or city, pays *an additional $9200* each year into his retirement fund so that he may retire after 20 years of service. That $9200 is not regarded as income to the policeman. He pays no income taxes on it, even though it is deposited into the retirement fund for his benefit. If instead, he were paid the full $32,200 directly, the tax due on the additional income of $9200 would be about $3500. Through the retirement plan, the full $9200 is permitted to grow through dividents or interest, which are also free of income taxes.

Until the end of 1966, these tax benefits were available only to the employees of large organizations with pension plans. In that year, the Self-Employed Individuals Tax Retirement Act, popularly known as the Keogh Plan, and later the Employee Retirement Income Security Act of 1974, known as the Pension Reform Act, were passed.

These acts attempted to provide some of the tax-shelter benefits to the self-employed and to employees not covered by company pension plans. Basically, under an approved Keogh

Plan, 15% of earned income or $7500 a year, whichever is less, can now be salted away toward retirement, with annual contributions and interest earned free of current income taxes. An Individual Retirement Account (I.R.A.) is different from Keogh Plans. If a person is not covered by a retirement or pension plan where he or she works, that person can contribute to his or her I.R.A. 15% of earned income to a maximum of $1500 per year. An employee who earns, for example, $8000, can contribute $1200 toward his or her I.R.A.—provided he or she is not a participent in a company pension plan.

Both the Keogh and I.R.A. plans have advantages and disadvantages which should be weighed carefully.

The obvious advantage of both plans is the ability to deduct from current taxable income whatever is contributed into the plan in accordance with the stated limitations. In addition, as the contributions earn dividends or interest, these earnings are not taxed when earned. Since contributions to the funds are not reduced by current taxes, more money goes into the funds as principal, on which interest is earned, than would go into one's own savings accounts, deposits in which are first reduced by income taxes.

Not so obvious are the disadvantages.

Although a self-employed individual may simultaneously have more than one Keogh Plan in operation, he can switch funds from one plan to another only with the consent of the plan's custodian. Custodians for Keogh Plans are invariably banks or insurance companies. We know of a case where a man attempted to have the custodian of his Keogh Plan switch his funds from a low-paying regular savings account into higher-paying term certificates, since he couldn't touch the money until retirement in any case. The custodian, one of New York's savings banks, refused.

The I.R.A. does not present this difficulty. Tax-free withdrawals of any or all accumulated funds (contributions plus interest) from an I.R.A. are permitted, provided that the amount of the withdrawal is reinvested in another I.R.A. (or qualified pension plan of a new employer) within 60 days after the withdrawal.

Another disadvantage: Should you need any of the money in a retirement account before reaching age 59½, except for death or disability, heavy penalties are assessed.

Furthermore, since neither contributions nor interest earned thereon were subject to income taxes during the working years, they become subject to income taxes upon retirement in accordance with special rules. It is assumed that one's tax bracket will be lower after retirement. However, if funds have been deposited in Keogh or I.R.A. plans for many years, it is possible that the tax levied on the funds upon retirement will be higher than the tax would have been during one's earlier years of work.

Before subscribing to any promoted Keogh Plan or I.R.A., it would be wise to obtain detailed information about, *and up-to-date interpretations of*, the Pension Reform Act. Good sources of information include your accountant, publications of the U.S. Government Printing Office, the Internal Revenue Service, your Congressman, or your local library.

Those who select either a Keogh or I.R.A. plan may be interested to know that many of the money market funds, including the Reserve Fund and Money Market Management, have provisions for both plans. If the high earnings record of this type of fund is more attractive than bank interest, a call or postcard to any of the funds will bring full information and necessary forms.

In a larger sense, it should be of interest to examine carefully the impact of any legislation that permits income to be exempt or sheltered from taxation.

Under the Pension Reform Act of 1974, many millions of people will put many billions of dollars into Keogh and I.R.A.

plans, will reduce their taxable incomes by those billions, and therefore pay some billions less in taxes to federal and state governments.

These amounts, impressive as they may be, are only a small fraction of the amounts that go into regular non-Keogh or I.R.A. pension, retirement, and profit-sharing plans that are as tax-sheltered as are the Keogh and I.R.A. plans. All types of pension plans combined account for the removal of scores of billions of dollars of income from the base upon which income taxes are levied. As an example, more than a quarter of a *billion* dollars ($270,000,000) is put, tax-free, each year into the pension plans for just the 30,000 policemen of New York City and neighboring Long Island. Add in all the sums paid into the pension plans of all of the rest of the nation's civil servants, large company employees and executives, and the amount that is removed from the taxable base is mind-boggling!

On top of this vast sum exempt from taxes, interest is earned each year on the contributions to pension funds for all the previous years, plus interest on top of all the interest previously accrued. This, too, escapes taxation.

Parenthetically, it should be noted that the national retirement system, Social Security, does not offer the employee the advantage of tax-sheltering of income put into the Fund. F.I.C.A. (Social Security) deductions from the paycheck are *not* deductible! However, the important question to examine is: Does this type of tax benefit for pension fund participants really help the tax-paying employee?

Governments do not reduce their expenditures because tax breaks have been given to some favored group; the same amount of money must be raised through taxes. This is easily accomplished by increasing the *rate* of taxation. With or without tax-shelter or exemption on income put into retirement funds, taxpayers end up paying the *same amount* in taxes!

Why, then, do our Congressmen enact such legislation? Among the many possible reasons, a few stand out.

It makes the Congress appear to be giving us something for nothing. We think that through tax exemption we pay less taxes. That something-for-nothing line is very appealing.

The granting of tax-shelter for retirement funds does not reduce the amount of money the government collects, but it does guarantee that there will be income which the government can and will tax when the pension funds are finally paid out to the retired.

The Pension Act does, perhaps, stimulate the economy, albeit in a perverse way. It gives additional work to I.R.S. men, accountants, the advertising industry, and numerous other non-productive elements. It also engenders kilotons of printed material from the banks and insurance companies that push their plans and provides the postal service with additional billions of pieces of mail to deliver.

The entire concept of granting tax exemptions very possibly amounts to no more than putting money into one pocket and taking it out of the other. The one constructive feature of the Pension Reform Act is that it induces people to save for retirement.

However, our preoccupation with retirement is fast creating an impracticable, unmanageable, self-defeating monster. Most of us are productive members of society for about 45 years, with an average of a score of years devoted to childhood and education and perhaps five to 10 years of retirement. However, organized groups with the power to enforce their demands have been able to reduce materially their working years and thus increase their work-free retirement period.

Policemen in the greater New York area now achieve full retirement after 20 years of work. That means that, of approximately 70 years, 20 are productive and 50 nonproductive. And recent Police Benevolent Association contracts call for four days of work, then 96 hours off duty, and all that on top of very liberal vacation time and sick leave.

I live in Nassau County, Long Island, in New York State. Among the county, city, and village police forces, 4,000 patrolmen are employed. Adding in neighboring Suffolk County's policemen, a total of some 7,500 men in blue earn their livings from the public treasuries.

The average policeman—not including sargeants and higher officers, just the cop on the beat—earns $23,800 in cash wages —plus $11,900 in the cost of fringe benefits—to a total cost of $35,700 per man and woman.

For this, the officer works 191 shifts a year to a total of 1,358 hours—equivalent to 34 40-hour weeks with 18 weeks (or four months) off for vacation and sick leave. He earns $17.50 for each hour worked plus $9 per hour in fringe benefits, to a total cost to the taxpayer of $26.50 for every hour that a policeman works.

One fringe benefit the man in blue receives is of interest to us. The municipality pays into the retirement plan for each and every policeman *more than* $9,500 per year—or $7 per hour. It is these payments that make it possible for our "finest" to enjoy "20 and out," their jargon for retirement after 20 years of 34 weeks each. (The total of 780 weeks is about equivalent to 16 years of the average American's working life.)

Were we all to achieve this utopian level, our combined productive capacities could not possibly supply us with the necessities and luxuries we have come to expect. We cannot all be parasites for 50 of 70 years. If we were all as successful as the police, our standard of living should reach the equivalent of that of the aborigines of Australia.

Are there other reasons why our legislators pass such laws as the two pension acts? Try this on for size.

Notice that you cannot manage your own retirement fund. The laws require that either a bank or insurance company act as trustee or custodian. In either case, for all practical purposes, you have little or no control. The result is that the vast majority of the many billions of *your* retirement monies are given to privately owned, privately operated banks. With the connivance of the federal regulatory agencies, the banks pay for your money at preposterously niggardly rates. Then the banks turn around and charge borrowers enough for *your* money to keep their executives in chauffeured limousines, their owners in private jets, and their employees in thousands of gleaming new edifices that rival, although perhaps crassly, the Taj Mahal.

Perhaps it is only incidental that pension reform has resulted in a several hundred billion dollar giveaway to bankers. But a giveaway it still is.

And the irony of it all is that we are convinced that Pension Reform Acts are progressive social legislation!

However, like it or not, Keogh and I.R.A. are probably here to stay. And anyone who can take advantage of these pension plans is a fool if he doesn't. Every taxpayer pays for them (in higher tax rates), so you might as well enjoy their benefits.

9.

The Greatest Battle of All

The greatest danger to financial security and even our basic freedoms is continuing inflation. Realistically—and rightly—it has been likened to a state upon which war must be declared.

This great land has been plagued by constantly increasing prices for more than a quarter century. During that time, the cost of a subway or bus ride, the daily newspaper, bread and rolls, a college education, or a hospital stay have increased in price approximately ten-fold. It should not be necessary to warn that if we continue riding this road to disaster, 25 years hence prices will be at least 10 (if not many more) times as high as they are now. It is only during the last decade that the general public has become aware of the insidious effects of constant cost escalation. Recall that President Johnson attempted to hold the line at a 3% rate by "jawboning." Before we knew it, we suffered through "double digit inflation," and it may come again —soon. Most of us buy, consume, and waste more of everything than we need—food, clothing, shelter, vehicles, appliances, toiletries, energy, entertainments—necessities, luxuries, and frivolities. If this were the 1920s, '30s, or '40s, inflation could be halted by decreasing our buying. In the "old" days, lowered demand brought prices down, a phenomenon sometimes called the controls of the marketplace. Or the supply of money and credit could be reduced, which would also force prices downward. But no longer—not today—and not for the past 25 years.

We have gone through periods of decreased demand, recessions, tight money policy, and "money crunches," but there has been no halt to the upward movement of prices. An entire generation has never experienced price stability.

Recall that the economists' definition of inflation is:

> Disproportionate and relatively sharp and sudden *increase in the quantity of money or credit,* or both, relative to goods available for purchase. *Inflation always produces* a rise in the price level.

We have witnessed several *reductions* in the quantity of money and credit, yet there has been no halt to price increases. Likewise, the controls of the marketplace have been ineffective as a brake on price spirals, as indicated by the continued inflation during recessions.

To find a cure for the plague of inflation, it is necessary first to determine why the previously effective medicines no longer work, why the virus has developed an immunity to the time-honored cures.

The search for the "why" brings us back to the year 1951. One of the country's largest industrial giants had endured a months-long strike of its employees seeking wage increases of something less than 2%. Management knew that their company enjoyed the greatest demand in history for its many products. The strike-forced shutdown caused the loss of hundreds of millions in sales, business which went to traditional competitors and dozens of fledgling manufacturers whose success was assured by the unanticipated strike-induced sales boom. With settlement and resumption of full-scale operations, management came to a decision that was to have far-reaching effects on our and other free world economies for a generation or more. Henceforth, management was to anticipate the demands of labor—and meet those demands so that not a day, not an hour, would be lost due to labor strife.

This novel approach to labor relations was brilliantly simple if not Machiavellian. The increased cost of labor would be passed on to the consumer, along with overhead and profit on the additional cost. Thus, profit margins would be maintained. The company reasoned (correctly) that its competition would be forced to pay comparably increased labor costs and would likewise have to increase prices. Since demand at that time seemed inexhaustible, sales would not suffer, while increased prices would mean increased profits and increased gross sales figures. Higher gross and net profits would increase the value of the stock of the company; the price of its securities would soar. (They did!) And with the stockholders happy, management would rest secure. Last, but by no means least, increased wages would make labor happy. More important, labor *leaders* would be happy because, having gotten more and more for their membership, the labor bosses would also rest secure.

Management of this industrial empire had found the magic formula. It worked—for decades. Naturally, management elsewhere followed suit. Soon demands went from less than 2% to 4%, then 5%. And as increased prices took away whatever seemed to have been gained from increased wages, labor's needs went to 10%, then 20%, and 30%.

Civil servants across the nation eyed their industrial brethren with envy—and promptly closed ranks and strengthened their heretofore impotent unions. And they found that they had even more clout than their industrial counterparts. Try running a country without mail delivery or a city without transportation, or garbage removal, or police, or firemen. City halls counted the votes of organized labor—and promptly surrendered. Before long many of these civil servants insisted on, and got, "4 & 96," jargon for 96 hours off after 4 days of work, and "20 and out," which means retirement after 20 years service regardless of age. And unlimited sick leave, more vacation pay, more paid holidays.

So labor got—or seemed to get—more and more, while they

worked and produced less and less. But management always kept a jump ahead of labor. By the formula invented by the industrial giant, prices went up, up, and away—so labor's gains were, to a great extent, in dollars, but not in purchasing power.

Some industries eventually found that the controls of the marketplace were adversely affecting them; their goods would not sell at the necessarily inflated prices. Imports were cheaper. So factories closed and unemployment reared its ugly head. Carpets, shoes, radio and television, calculators, cars, clothing; multinational companies found it cheaper and better to produce elsewhere and import the merchandise into the U.S. Small manufacturers folded their tents and silently stole away. Still using their well-known American brand names, entire industries moved their production facilities to the Far East and, to a lesser extent, Western Europe. (Try finding a radio made in the U.S.A.)

Dollars fled the country to pay for foreign produced goods. At the same time, with regularly increased prices, American manufacturers lost much of their traditional export markets: electronics, automobiles, steel, shipbuilding, power plants—to name but a few.

With export markets denied and imports increasing, unemployment became our steady companion. And the value of the inflated U.S. dollar tumbled—relative to buying power, or gold, or currencies of nations that were able, competitively, to balance imports with exports.

Despite this gloomy picture, business as a whole did not do badly—except, of course, for the increased number of business failures. And labor did well for itself, too. There is no question but that the unionized worker lives far better today than he did 25 years ago—provided that he hasn't involuntarily been recruited to the army of unemployed.

Mathematics and logic tell us that the cycle of increasing prices and wages should be self-defeating, that a bust should result. Yet the economy continued to survive, punctuated by only minor recessions, for more than a quarter century. The time honored 14-year cycles of boom and bust no longer occurred. Searching for reasons for this economic survival over so long a period, we find that both our economy and our inflation have been subsidized. The subsidies came from two major sources.

Gradually, over a 20-year period, our economy stole away the buying power of a tremendous mass of capital; capital that consisted of the people's savings, stock investments, fixed retirement funds, and insurance policies. That entire mass of capital today can buy only 10% or 12% of what it could have bought before the inflation. However, the owners of this capital, the common people, were helpless to do anything about the rape of their resources, so the plunder continued. But not so with the second source of our economic subsidy.

For two decades, through our "economic imperialism," we were able to keep the costs of most of our raw materials from increasing at anything near the rate of our own price increases. Whether we look at oil or sugar or coffee, or any of the ores mined in the multitude of underdeveloped areas of the world, by comparison to our price escalation, that part of our production cost remained relatively stable. Then the situation reversed. No longer can we buy at the price *we* want to pay. Our inflated, devalued dollars are no longer that desirable. We pay *their* price —and now, finally, that price threatens to keep pace with our inflation.

More than $25 billion a year net leaves this country to pay for our importing binge—a figure that would be markedly reduced, if not wiped out, if American business and labor could compete with the rest of the world as it once did but no longer can. Meanwhile, much of that $25 billion a year is coming back home—but at an awesome price. As has been happening in England, foreign interests are gradually buying and gaining control of some of the most productive capacities of this country. Every day we sell off more.

Those who may have had a gnawing suspicion that business, particularly big business, has had unduly strong influence over our governmental bodies and the law-making process, shudder at the thought of what will happen when that business is controlled from non-democratic, feudal, or totalitarian shores.

Something must be done, and time is not on our side.

Let us look back in time. Societies, from primitive to modern, always supported a privileged class. Hundreds of years ago the nobility, the clergy, and the military were "privileged," and could extract from society all that society had to offer, paid for through the combined labor of the great masses. Everyone had to donate part of the fruits of their toil to maintain the privileged class in style, supplying their needs, wants, desires. But those privileged classes were only a tiny percentage of the total population, 2% supported by the extra labor of 98% of the people.

Privileged classes expanded during the heydays of empires, both Roman and British. In the former, captured slaves and exploited colonies were what made it possible, while in the latter, the natural wealth of the far-flung colonial empire and low paid labor subsidized the multiplication of the privileged.

For perhaps a hundred years we, without colonies, were able to accomplish much the same as the English, through the combination of a hard-work ethic and economic, if not political, domination of less developed areas of the world which were the sources of much of our raw materials and edibles. In addition, as the country grew, we were able to maintain countless sources of cheap (if not slave) immigrant labor.

But no more. Rome has no slaves. England no colonies, and we no sources of cheap materials and labor. Even the migrant farm workers are organizing, protected by laws.

During the last quarter century, the seat of power shifted from capital alone to a combination of capital (including the newly-formed "managerial class") and organized labor. In the last five or six years, the power center has again shifted, this time to include those who control sources of basic materials, particularly in the less developed areas of the world. Now, the decisions in Brazil, Iran, or Saudi Arabia affect us as much as those of the AFL-CIO. In humanistic terms, this broadening of the power base is good. As labor successfully fought for a bigger share of the economic pie, so too did the backward, exploited peoples—or probably more realistically, their leaders.

The economic pie grows only with increased productivity due to technology and/or more productive labor. When one group is able to get a larger slice of the pie, that larger increment must come from somewhere else. If it comes from increased productivity, other groups sharing the pie continue to recieve the *same amount* of pie, but their *percentage* of the total pie is *decreased*. However, when the larger bite is greater than can be supplied by increased productivity, someone else has to pay; that is, other groups must be satisfied with less, in order to supply a larger share to another.

By means of diagrams, admittedly oversimplified, let us look at what has happened to the economic pie since the start of the second half of the twentieth century. This examination may offer us clues by which our system may be saved from potential disaster.

Figure 19. Division of Economic Pie, circa 1951
(Buying Power, arbitrarily divided into four equal shares for simplicity.)

By the end of two decades of generally increasing prices and wages, as well as increased productivity and Gross National Product, the shares of the economic pie had changed. Note that the total pie is larger by 1971 than it was in 1951.

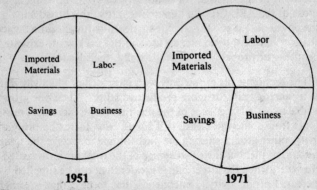

1951   **1971**

Figure 20. Division of Economic Pie, 1951 & 1971.

During this period (approximately 1951-1971), people on fixed retirement incomes, beneficiaries of life insurance policies, and the general public with savings in banks and bonds watched helplessly while, at their expense, business and labor helped themselves to larger and larger shares of the total pie. Suppliers of raw materials, etc., were in the same boat. The prices they received per ton or gallon for what they sold to the U.S. went up (for example) 14% while the value of the dollars they received went down 80%.

Then, starting about 1973-74, the worm turned. Oil exporting nations organized—followed by their sugar and coffee producing third world cousins. Almost overnight, prices of imported materials doubled, tripled, quadrupled. The balance swung somewhat in their favor, but not to the extent to which business and labor had ravaged the pie.

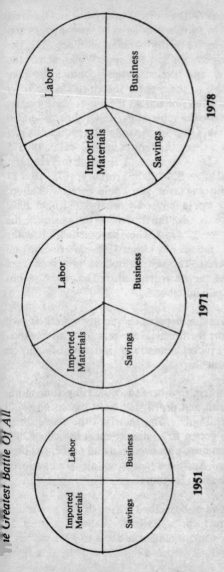

Key: Imported Materials — Oil, sugar, coffee, ores, minerals, etc.
Labor — Industry and government, productive and nonproductive.
Savings — Cash, savings accounts, life insurance, bonds, annuities.
Business — Investment capital and management.

Figure 21. Division of Economic Pie, 1951, 1971, 1978.

From 1951 through 1973, the gains of both labor and business were paid for literally by foreign producers of raw materials and consumables and the native thrifty population. Since 1973, the foreign producers joined labor and business. While each of the three—labor, business, and foreign cartels—continues to take larger and larger shares of the pie, the increments come from those who have saved a few dollars. As the power block creates more and more inflation, the value of the dollar shrinks—much faster than interest makes it grow. Anyone who thinks this picture is exaggerated can check the figures at his local bank: $75 invested in a ($100) U.S. Government E Bond in February, 1951, could be cashed in for $224.20 in February, 1978, after 27 years. After average income taxes, you would be left with about $180. But that $180 would buy only what $20 would have bought in 1951! Not only have the thrifty *not* been paid for the use of their savings for 27 years, they have actually had the value of these savings reduced by about 75%—after adding all the compounded interest. The savings dollars have subsidized what has been called the unwritten, unspoken, unholy conspiracy between capital and labor.

For generations, working people believed it was in their own best interest to support the financial aspirations of all workers. They wouldn't cross a picket line and remained unflinchingly on the side of labor against capital.

And every time workers anywhere succeeded in getting more, the cost, plus overhead and profit, has been passed on to all workers, to the general public. But that isn't the whole story. Every time labor has gotten 10%, management has taken 20% or 30%—and that cost also, plus overhead and profit, has been passed on to all of us. And even that is not all. We have been forced to pay for a helluva lot more!

Every time a football or basketball player signs a new multi-million dollar contract, or a Barbara Walters captures $5 million, or a Johnny Carson obtains a boost to $2½ million a year, or a Muhammad Ali garners $9 or $12 million for a fight, not only the sports fan(atic), Tonight Show devotee, or news junkie must pay for it, but the general public must as well. Why? Because the networks include these costs in computing their advertising rates to their service and manufacturing industry clients—which they in turn add on to the price of their products. You may never have seen a boxing match or football game, but you have paid for them and the astronomical earnings of their stars—by having the value of your dollars shrink because of increased prices due to increased cost of advertising as well as labor and management.

So why not wage and price controls? That would stop the wage-price spiral. But it's an old story. Business might like wage controls but won't live with price controls. Labor loves frozen prices but will not abide a wage freeze. And management (as well as overpaid celebrities) will have no part of controlled executive salaries and fringe benefits. So controls are the kind of hot potato politicians avoid like the plague. What's more, there are other drawbacks to long-term controls, as we learned during World War II and the Korean War, times when the people of the country were welded together in common cause, unlike today, when our only interest seems to be ''What's in it for me?'' Controls spawn gray and black markets, as does rationing.

On the surface, without price controls, it appears that inflation will continue for the next quarter century as it has for the past. So, just as the 2¢ newspaper is now 10 times that price at 20¢, and the 5¢ bus ride is 50¢, so, by 25 years from now, the paper will be $2 and the fare $5. At least that is what will happen if there are still subsidies available with which to underwrite inflation—as there were in the form of cheap imports and depletion of the value of savings.

However, foreign suppliers will no longer deplete their precious natural resources in return for worthless dollars. As dollar value declines, materials cost will go up proportionately. And savings dollars cannot be raped for too much longer. No, the kind of inflation we have had probably cannot go on for another 10 years, much less 25. The odds are that we will have a big bust well before we reach 2000, and a good chance it will hit before 1984. Then, a military dictator will probably arrive on his white horse to "save" us. It would be well to remember that political anarchy has always brought repression. The uncontrolled ability of business and labor and management and foreign cartels to take whatever they want is nothing short of economic anarchy—and the eventual result will be repression, economic and political.

If we want to keep our freedoms, we had better do something, and quickly. Time has almost run out. But what can we do?

First, if we examine what occurred during the 90-day wage-price freeze of the first Nixon administration, we find that much of business managed to raise prices by changing name, packaging, trim, or through other loopholes. Only wages were actually frozen. Price-wage freezes usually end up as wage controls only. This is not the answer.

Currently, moral persuasion is proposed. Everyone is for morality—for the other guy. Unfortunately (but realistically), there is as much chance of moral persuasion being successful as there was of President Johnson's "jawboning" being effective—none.

Perhaps we should look back to the management decision of 1951. Consider its effects and how readily all of business jumped onto the bandwagon of "give labor whatever it wants and raise the price accordingly," or, "why fight labor; if you can't lick 'em, join 'em." With union-enforced, industry-wide wage standards, there has been no incentive to resist the increase of production costs due to higher wages. If anything, just the reverse has been true. The more business paid labor, the more profit it made.

We have gone so long and so deep in the price-wage whirlpool that no one knows who is ahead. Labor says it needs more now to make up for already extant price increases, and business maintains price increases are justified to account for recent labor and current raw material and energy increases.

Both labor and business are subverting their own aspirations by continuing with the cycle. Both probably realize it, yet neither can unilaterally stop. Both should wake up to the possibility that if they continue, tranquility may be *forced* upon both—the economic tranquility of today's USSR, or worse.

Till now, the ability to raise wages, seemingly at will, appears to have been profitable to labor. Likewise, the ability to increase prices has, in the main, been profitable to business. It is too late for business to regret the monster it has created.

Why not try to find some way to make price and wage increases *un*profitable to both business and labor—by giving business the financial incentive to resist *any* cost increases. And by giving labor the ability to get more—more goods and services —for their dollars, not more dollars. If such a formula could be found, prices would stay level or recede and the value of the dollar would go up.

Following is one suggestion that might conceivably bring the miracle to pass.

Background Information

Sometime in the 1960s, the XYZ Corp. produced 10 million thingamajigs which it sold for $10 each. Thus:

Sales	=	$100,000,000
Cost of production (overhead included)	=	90,000,000
Profit before taxes	=	10,000,000 (10% of sales)
Taxes	=	5,000,000
Net profit after taxes	=	$ 5,000,000 (5% of sales)

Some years later, the same company still produced the same number of the same item, but costs had gone up so that the price of the item was then $20—or double the previously listed price. Thus:

Sales	=	$200,000,000
Cost of production	=	180,000,000
Profit before taxes	=	20,000,000 (10% of sales)
Taxes	=	10,000,000
Net profit after taxes	=	$ 10,000,000 (5 % of sales)

Note that, although sales and profits doubled, profit as a percent of sales remained the same. However, the value (buying power) of the $10 million profit was no greater than when the profit was half that, or $5 million, because the value of the dollar had shrunk to half its previous value—the inevitable result of inflation. The position of the company had not changed; it was not hurt in any way by inflation. If, on the other hand, the company had resisted production-cost increases, it would have been faced with a shutdown and consequent loss of business. It was more profitable to pay increased costs and raise prices. The company had no incentive to resist cost increases.

During this period in which prices doubled, some costs did not double while others more than doubled, for example:

Wages (approximately) doubled, but, in addition, labor received more and better fringe benefits, such as increased vacations, sick time, medical benefits, and earlier and better retirement plans. So, the standard of living of labor improved.

Likewise, management bettered their lot. Their salaries more than doubled and, as frosting for the cake, legislators obligingly reduced the top Federal income tax brackets from 70% to 50%. They *really* did well.

Meanwhile, the costs of energy, telephone, and raw materials increased significantly less than 100%. Improved technology made it possible for communications to operate profitably at less than general price increases, but with energy, oil, and raw materials, it was necessary for suppliers to sell more of their precious, irreplaceable natural resources in order to maintain their buying power.

And as the price of a thingamajig went from $10 to $20, the value of the dollar dropped by 50%. The real value of savings, annuities, bonds, life insurance policies, and fixed pensions was cut in half. Ouch!

With this background, what can be done, short of a controlled economy, to prevent the continued inflation and consequent devaluation of the people's life savings? The answer might come by finding a way to penalize those segments of business and labor that participate in the inflationary cycle, and *reward* those that do not, with even greater reward to those who help reverse the cycle. And it can be done!

Aware of it or not, labor is already penalized to some extent by inflation. If wages and prices double, under the present graduated income tax, labor's spendable income does not double, because the higher wages presumably fall into higher income tax brackets—if deductions and exclusions are not periodically raised.

But business is not so penalized. Their tax is not graduated (and probably could not be). The same yardstick cannot or should not be applied to a billion dollar business as to a million dollar one, except as it is now done through practically straight line rather than graduated taxation.

However, there is a way to apply equitably a system of graduated taxation on business, and by so doing, real financial reward—as well as penalty—could be built in through several steps of taxation and rebates or credits. Business as a whole might pay the same amount of taxes, but distribution would be more equitable and, most importantly, business would have financial reasons to keep costs and prices down.

Under present corporate tax regulations, virtually the same tax is paid by each of two companies earning (for example) $20 million before taxes, even though one of the corporations may represent an investment ten times larger than the other.

Step 1. First, instead of levying taxes based solely on total profit, taxes should be applied on the basis of *profit per unit of net asset value.* Some initial percentage of profit (profit as a percent of net assets, not profit as a percent of gross business) could be exempt from corporate income taxes. Profits in excess of the exempt percentage would be taxed on a graduated, increasing scale.

Under this proposed tax, the company with the larger net assets would pay less taxes on the same *amount* of profit, because its profit as a percent of investment (net asset value) would be less than that of the company with a smaller net asset value.

Next, it should be recognized that some industries present higher risks to investors than others, and that greater returns for such higher risks are both justified and necessary in order to encourage investments. Furthermore, and even more importantly, the second step would *penalize* participation in an inflationary cycle while the third step would give monetary reward for participation in a *deflationary* cycle.

A base period (of perhaps five, seven, or 10 years) would be chosen. Assume the base period is seven years. From previously filed accounting statements and tax returns, the profit (or loss) per unit of net asset value for each of the seven years would be computed for every corporation. From this, the *average base period profit* per unit of assets would be calculated.

This second step consists of two taxes in addition to that in the first step:

Step 2, Part A. In any year, profits (per unit of net assets, or PUNA) in excess of the *average base period profit* would be taxed on a graduated, increasing scale.

Step 2, Part B. In any year, profits (PUNA) in excess of profit (PUNA) earned in the *most profitable of the seven base period years* would be additionally taxed on a graduated scale.

> The proposed Step 2 penalizes inflation-produced profits, while both Steps 1 *and* 2 encourage capital investment because such investment results in the lowering of tax brackets in both steps.

The third step consists of two tax credit or rebate sections:

Step 3, Part A. In any year, profits (PUNA) less than the *average base period profit* would receive a tax credit (or rebate) on a graduated, increasing scale.

Step 3, Part B. In any year, profits (PUNA) less than those earned in the *least profitable of the seven base period years* would receive a tax credit (or rebate) on a graduated, increasing scale.

> The proposed Step 3 rewards deflation-produced profit decreases and partially subsidizes business losses. As do the first two steps, the third step encourages capital improvement and investment.
>
> In practice, Steps 2 and 3 would be combined, creating a positive or negative tax on business, depending upon whether profits (per unit of net assets) increased or decreased.

A few other items should be considered in combination with the proposed three-step tax program.

At present, when a stock issue is floated to obtain working capital (thus increasing investment and net asset value), that capital is paid for by means of dividends (and, supposedly, equity in the company). Taxes are levied on profits *before* the dividends are paid out. However, instead of issuing stock, if a company borrows money (e.g., from banks, or by issuing debenture bonds or selling commercial paper), that money is paid for by interest—which is considered a cost of doing business and therefore paid (and deducted) before profits, which are taxable, are computed. This unequal treatment of operating funds results in double taxation on dividends (corporate plus personal income tax) but only single taxation on interest.

Under the proposed three-step tax, payment of dividends would decrease net asset value, thereby increasing profit per unit of net assets and increasing the tax. On the other hand, profits retained and not paid out as dividends would increase net asset value, thereby decreasing profit per unit of net assets, thus decreasing the tax. It seems likely that under my proposed tax system all, or at least part, of dividend payments could be considered part of business cost and therefore exempt from business taxes. Dividend income would, of course, be subject to personal income taxes, as it is now.

It is necessary that a brake be applied to the inordinate and unilateral skyrocketing salary increases given by management to management—as well as the ability of the "celebrity class" to demand and get whatever they please and *still* receive preferential tax treatment. Explanation: Until several years ago, the top fedeal income tax bracket was 70%. Then, our pressure sensitive government *reduced* the top bracket on *earned* income from 70% to 50%—while the 70% remained for unearned income. Overnight, those salaries of $500,000 or $2.5 million were worth about 65% more. Likewise with those multi-million dollar prize-fight fees. Meanwhile, that loss in tax revenues was made up to the Treasury, as made up it had to be, by us, the general inflation-robbed public in the lower tax brackets.

So, if taxes are to be reformed, earned income tax brackets should be returned to 70%. However, the management class could merely raise their salaries to compensate for the renewed taxes unless such moves are made difficult. Perhaps corporate salaries in excess of some figure—say $100,000 or $150,000—should not be considered a cost of doing business, but rather consider the amount in excess of the set limits as a non-deductible contribution. Such a move might discourage inordinate and unrestrained robbery of corporate treasuries.

In addition, consideration should be given to increasing personal income tax brackets to perhaps 90%, but with "tax averaging" permitted both backward and forward for some extended period like 10 years each way for a total of 20 years, or even longer, to protect those with high earning abilities that endure for only limited periods of time—such as athletes, artists, actors and, yes, executives. Thus, a high income of short duration during a lifetime could be spread out over at least 20 (and preferably more) years.

The proposed tax revisions tend to discourage business, management, and the privileged from participating in the quarter-century cycle of inflation. But labor is not completely blameless. Therefore, lastly, the practice of annually increasing tax exemptions and deductions, as well as the sometime increasing of the amount earnable within a tax bracket, should be stopped. Permitting higher dollar income without increasing the taxes thereon in effect gives the government's blessing to the inflationary cycle.

But let's be practical. No President will ask for, nor will a Congress legislate, so sweeping a tax revision and inflation-controlling measure. However, it would be politically and logistically practical to phase in gradually a program such as this. Why not, as a start for the first year, reduce the business tax by one-fourth (from 48% to 36%), and add a tax on Profits per Unit of Net Assets to recover the tax revenue lost by the 25% business tax reduction. Then, in the following years, reduce the business tax further and raise the PUNA tax until the archaic, inflation-rewarding, straight-line profits tax is eliminated, replaced by the inflation-controlling tax on profits per unit of net assets.

Were the proposed tax revision enacted, it would be comparatively simple for the government's computers to determine what the tax rates in each bracket should be for both business and individual income, in order to raise the necessary revenues. The higher the tax rates, the higher the tax credits and rebates; so, by raising tax rates, business is encouraged to cash in on tax rebates, discouraged from fostering inflation, and rewarded for achieving revaluation (deflation). Prices might well start moving downward, thereby offering labor more for static earnings rather than less for increased earnings. And, once again, the U.S. dollar might become a reasonably stable world standard of value.

If wealth and financial security is your goal, inflation is your bggest enemy. Invest your time, your thoughts, your energies into devising ways in which that enemy can be overcome. The tax revisions herein proposed constitute but one suggestion.

It took a dozen years of hard work by dedicated people to get Proposition 13 passed in California. Now, finally, legislators are starting to understand the mood of the electorate. Possibly the best investment you could make would be 45¢—for postage on three letters: one to your Congressman, and one each to your two Senators—insisting that they give top priority to stopping inflation. Give them your suggestions—or refer them to this chapter.

Historical Appendix

A. The Origin Of Money

Money? Love of it is said to be the root of all evil. Perhaps. But undeniably money—love it or not—is needed for housing, food, clothing, transportation, and dozens of other items for sustenance and comfort. Few, though, despite their interest in increasing their stockpile of it, ever stop to think what money really is, much less how it has changed over time.

Early civilizations bartered goods and services for other goods and services. To escape the obvious limitations of barter, man invented a standard of exchange. It first took the form of cattle, grain, axes, skins, and many other items of value. By the 12th Century B.C. these real items were replaced by miniature bronze replicas of the originals. Thus, if an ox was equivalent to 20 axes *or* 50 pounds of grain, the miniature bronze ox could be used to buy, for example, 10 axes *and* 25 pounds of grain.

Figure 1. Roman Quadrussis (4 asses), 6th Cent. B.C.E.

It wasn't until the 7th Century B.C.E. that coins, as we know them, first appeared, and it took another 1800 years before paper money came into existence, in China. But both the paper money we use today, and modern banking, had their origins in England in the 14th to 17th centuries.

By that time, money had gained acceptance both as a medium of exchange (in lieu of barter) and as a standard of worth. Rare metals, gold and silver, were the basis of what is called "full bodied money." Each coin had a face value equal to the value of the gold or silver it contained. Paper money carried the guarantee that it could be converted into "full bodied money" or "specie."

In those times, the value of money remained reasonably stable because it either was or represented an item of intrinsic value—gold or silver—and was not produced by whim on a printing press.

However, all too often full bodied money did not serve the needs of a people or a nation. Many times in this country's history, payments in specie were suspended by the banks, and Scrip—promissory notes or "greenbacks"—were used instead. During the Civil War, the U.S. Treasury printed $400,000,000 in greenbacks, not backed by specie, and ordained them legal tender for the payment of all debts, public and private. It was not until 1879 that specie payments were resumed.

Nineteen hundred thirty three saw the abandonment of our gold standard, and with it the right to convert currency to gold at a pre-fixed rate. Now our coinage is "token coin," coins with face values greater than the value of the metal they contain, and our paper is "credit money" with a face value greater than the reserves that back it up.

B. What You Should Know About Banking

Banking is substantially a middle-man enterprise in which many small surpluses of money are gathered together in the form of deposits and loans through a promise of interest payments and the return of the principal at some future time. These gathered funds are then loaned out or otherwise invested at a rate of return at least high enough to pay interest to depositors, pay the costs of the operation, and absorb the risks of making loans.

Although the temples of Babylon made loans 4,000 years ago and private banking firms existed around 575 B.C., the true ancestors of the modern commercial banker were the English goldsmiths of the 12th to 14th Centuries who held people's gold and specie (solid gold and silver coin) for safekeeping at a fee. They issued notes to the depositor on the gold they held, notes that acknowledged receipt of specie by the goldsmith.

The 12th Century goldsmith may be likened to the 20th Century safe-deposit box. The "depositor" received no interest; he paid for the safekeeping service. In time, the goldsmith's notes, rather than the gold or coins they represented, were used to pay debts. Notes circulated instead of gold; the notes became the money of the time. They were seldom presented to the goldsmith for redemption. Therefore, the amount of gold and specie the goldsmiths held constantly increased.

By the 14th Century, the enterprising goldsmiths, realizing that they were the constant custodians of sizable hoards of gold, began issuing notes in excess of the real value of the gold supply each held. Of course, since the recipient of such a note had not deposited specie with the goldsmith, he was charged a fee or interest for the loan of the note.

Figure 2. Gold Coin (Specie), English Noble (Edward III, 1327-1377).

This changeover from the goldsmith's role as custodian to that of lender of funds owned by other people probably made the smith the first modern commercial banker and the originator of the *principal of credit based upon fractional reserves.*

The issuance of notes in amounts greater than the value of the gold supply that backed them made goldsmithing a very profitable—and sometimes dangerous—enterprise. Fees were charged depositors for the safekeeping service and interest was charged the borrowers of notes. However, the safekeeping service wasn't always safe.

In those violent years, in times of crisis, those who had deposited gold with the smith rushed to redeem their notes. But because of the issuance of credit based on fractional reserves, more notes were presented for redemption than the deposited gold could accommodate. This was the 14th Century version of a "run" on a bank and, no doubt, resulted in some of these early banker-goldsmiths being hung or drawn and quartered by irate depositors.

Today, depositors are in an even less secure position. They have no gold or specie; they *deposit* notes. Yes, notes. Look at any U.S. paper currency. it is engraved:

FEDERAL RESERVE NOTE
THE UNITED STATES OF AMERICA
ONE DOLLAR
THIS NOTE IS LEGAL TENDER FOR ALL DEBTS,
PUBLIC AND PRIVATE

Figure 3. Current Federal Reserve Note (Series 1963).

Now look at the dollar bill, series of 1957. See that the inscription is quite different:

SILVER CERTIFICATE
THIS CERTIFIES THAT THERE IS ON DEPOSIT
IN THE TREASURY OF THE UNITED STATES OF
AMERICA   ONE DOLLAR   IN SILVER PAYABLE
TO THE BEARER ON DEMAND

Photo courtesy of Harry J. Forman, Inc.

Figure 4. Silver Certificate (Series 1957).

That was when we were on a silver standard. Today, that 1957 silver dollar will bring four or five 1979 dollars.

And for the unkindest cut of all, look at the ten dollar certificate, series of 1928. Note the engraving on this collector's item:

THIS CERTIFIES THAT THERE HAVE BEEN DEPOSITED
IN THE TREASURY OF THE UNITED STATES OF AMERICA
TEN DOLLARS IN GOLD COIN PAYABLE TO THE BEARER
ON DEMAND   GOLD CERTIFICATE

Photo courtesy of Harry J. Forman, Inc.

Figure 5. Ten Dollar Gold Certificate (Series 1928).

Two of those Ten Dollar Gold Certificates, convertible into a $20 gold piece in 1932, are worth about $350 today. The dollars of the 20s and early 30s were worth 12 to 15 times what modern dollars are worth—and by the time you read these words, the ratio may well have reached 20 or 25 to 1.

This is of much more than academic interest. It should be a primary concern to those wanting financial security for themselves and their families. Ponder this for a moment: in less than 25 years, the cost (in our "soft," paper dollars) of many of the essentials of life has risen tenfold. The 2¢ daily newspaper is now 20¢, the nickel subway is 50¢, the $6,990 middle-class house in a nice neighborhood is $69,990. If you expect or hope to be alive 25 years from now, how does three quarters of a million dollars for a modest private one-family house strike you? Or $2.00 for your daily newspaper?

Everyone would like to see inflation just go away. But it won't. We're tired of hearing about it. We would rather *believe* the Administration's promises that inflation will be stopped or at least kept within "reasonable" bounds. Meanwhile, our worry is about the reappearance of double-digit inflation— 10% or more each year. Well, at a 10% rate, today's $69,990 house in 25 years will cost over $750,000! And if we are lucky, and the rate is held to 8%, that house will go for the bargain price of just under a half million dollars. How about only 5% inflation? *If* it can be done, and few are naive enough to believe it can, then the same house will cost only a little more than a quarter million!

HELPLESS, AREN'T WE?

No, not really. To help us overcome the ravages of inflation, we must maximize the earnings on our savings and, in the long run even more importantly, help initiate changes in our financial system so that inflation will become only a distasteful memory. To accomplish both ends, it is necessary that we know enough about the historical changes in financial systems to recognize not only the opportunities to make more money, but also to prevent glib talk and sleight-of-hand from robbing us of what we have worked so hard to amass. At a baseball game you may or may not be able to tell the players without a scorecard. In the financial game, however, without a rule book, you're sunk.

Though there is undoubtedly much room for improvement in a monetary system which fosters inflation and recession, great strides have been made since the days of the goldsmith who made loans against the pledge of material and property. Then, repayment was virtually assured; debtors defaulted under pain of imprisonment.

The early years of the American colonies witnessed a chronic shortage of money. This led to the founding of colonial banks which issued notes (in the form of loans) to the founders of the banks upon pledge to the banks of real estate as security for the notes issued. As the notes were printed and sent into circulation, there was no proportional increase in the amount of goods available, so prices for the same goods were bid higher. As more and more of this money (notes) circulated, further price inflation followed. Naturally, the land likewise went up in price, justifying additional loans and note issues which, in turn, put still more money into circulation—more money with which to bid for goods which had not increased in quantity. In an open market, the result then (as now) was increased prices for goods and services, or inflation caused by a sharp increase in the amount of money in circulation. To stifle the runaway inflation, the British Crown suppressed the land banks.

By comparison to the days of the Colonial Land Banks, credit today is easily available, merely on our promise to repay out of "anticipated" future earnings. Our version of the British Crown, the Federal Reserve Board, has, unfortunately, encouraged credit rather than suppressed it.

It may be well to repeat here the classic definition of inflation as found in dictionaries and economics texts. However, as has been demonstrated in the previous chapters, this definition is now, and has been for the past 20 years, only half true:

> **Inflation:** Disproportionate and relatively sharp and sudden increase in the quantity of money or credit, or both, relative to goods available for purchase. Inflation always *produces* a rise in the price level.

With the American Revolution, the need arose for a banking institution to help finance the war by making loans to the Continental Congress. In 1781, the Congress chartered the Bank of North America and subcribed to $250,000 of its $400,000 authorized capital. (A short time later, this first national bank obtained a charter from the State of Pennsylvania, because the authority of the Continental Congress to have granted the charter was questioned.) Although the Bank of North America was a private bank, it performed some of the functions of a central bank and prospered for over 80 years.

Figure 6. One-Penny Specie Note, Bank of North America, 1789.

Meanwhile, shortly after the end of the Revolutionary War, state banks were chartered by state legislatures and were permitted to issue loans (or notes) up to a fixed multiple of paid-in capital. Thus, as did the goldsmiths of the 14th Century, state banks issued notes based on fractional reserves. These banks profited and proliferated as the American economy expanded. Conversely, they helped the economy to grow by supplying the needed credit—credit in excess of their paid in capital.

In addition to the Bank of North America and state banks, in 1791 Congress created the first Bank of the United States to act as fiscal agent for the U.S. Government and to strengthen the market for government bonds so that the national government could assume the Revolutionary War debts of the individual states.

The bank's charter was for 20 years and authorized capital of $10 million, with the government subscribing to $2 million through payment with government bonds. The remaining capital participation was made available to the public, which had to subscribe at the rate of one-fourth in specie and three-fourths in 6% government bonds. The charter permitted the Bank of the U.S. to issue notes up to the amount of its capital, $10 million, but *not* a multiple of its capital as the state banks were permitted.

Figure 7. $30 Note, Bank of the U.S., 1791.

To play the money game successfully, it is important to understand monetary and banking systems, how they change with time to fulfill the needs of society, the unexpected as well as the planned effects on business and public.

Recall that the 14th Century goldsmith created credit in excess of the hard money supply (specie) by issuing notes in excess of his gold supply. This is referred to as *creating credit based on fractional reserves* because each note issued by the goldsmith was backed in gold by only a fraction of the face value of the note.

Next, the early colonial land banks created credit by issuing notes backed not by specie (gold), but by the value of the land. The more notes they issued, the more money circulated, forcing prices and land values upward, thereby justifying further note issues.

With nationhood, state banks appeared. They were authorized to, and did, issue notes—not just in excess of their paid-in capital (as the goldsmiths did), but to multiples of that capital. This expansion of credit made possible the post-war economic expansion.

Now let us examine the effect on the nation, the economy, and the banks, of the creation of the first Bank of the U.S.

First, to enable the U.S. Government to assume the war debts of the various states, the creation of the Bank of the U.S. made it possible for the Treasury to issue and sell $8 million in U.S. Bonds at an interest rate of 6%. Two of the eight million in bonds were put into the bank (as the government's investment). The public was permitted to subscribe to $8 million in bank shares. But to do so, for each dollar's worth of specie, the investor had to supply three dollars worth of government bonds. Therefore, the public subscribed to $8 million in bank shares by paying in $2 million in specie and $6 million in U.S. Bonds, which were purchased from the Treasury by the public for $6 million in specie.

What did this "manipulation" accomplish?

By creating the Bank of the U.S., the government collected $6 million in specie (from the public) which could be used to assume the states' war debt. It also owned 20% ($2 million of the $10 million in authorized capital) of the bank.

In counterbalance, the government owed the bondholders $10 million, to be repaid in the future, and the cost in interest at 6% was $600,000 per year. Both the annual interest cost and ultimate bond redemption would, of course, be raised by the taxing powers of the government.

The authorized capital or assets of the Bank of the U.S. consisted of the $2 million in specie (gold) and $8 million in government bonds. It was authorized to issue notes (which would be used as currency) up to $10 million.

The operations of the Bank of the U.S. were extremely successful and its notes became an important part of the money used, particularly by the business community. Its loans to business were an important factor in the rapid expansion of the economy in the early years of the nation, and its loans to the U.S. Treasury provided the central government with needed financing.

Investors in the bank were amply repaid. Throughout its 20-year history, annual dividends of 8% were declared, a return which materially increased the value of the investment. During the early years of the bank, the U.S. Government sold its shares (20%) at sufficient profit to repay the loans made by the bank to the Treasury.

As established, the first U.S. central bank, the first Bank of the United States, proved eminently successful during its entire history in fulfilling its objectives, which were:

1. To serve as fiscal agent of the U.S. Government, lending money to the government as needed;

2. To lend money to the business community;

3. To provide a money supply in the form of notes;

4. To strengthen the market for U.S. Government Bonds by its readiness to buy, sell, and hold U.S. obligations.

However, the first Bank of the U.S. failed to achieve permanence principally because of an accomplishment which it was not established to achieve, namely, the institution of a strict and inflexible control over the supply of money and credit. This central bank was not authorized to operate on a fractional reserve basis; it could issue notes only up to its $10 million authorized capital. But it also effectively limited fractional reserve credit operations by state banks.

By 1811, there were 88 state banks, each able to issue notes in excess of its capital. Whenever state bank notes came into the possession of the Bank of the U.S., it demanded prompt redemption in specie. If notes were not redeemable in specie, the Bank of the U.S. refused to accept them. The result was that state banks could issue no more in notes than they could redeem in specie. Thus, the Bank of the U.S. effectively prohibited the issuance of state bank notes on a fractional reserve basis, severely restricting credit at a time of burgeoning trade and production.

This credit-limiting policy antagonized the population and particularly the state banks which had strong Congressional influence. Compounding this resentment, after the government had sold its shares in the bank, it was charged that the bank established a chartered monopoly for a group of wealthy, privileged investors, with all the risks underwritten by the name and credit of the government, a monopoly which not only curtailed the supply of credit, but competed with state banks whose successful operation it undermined by effectively controlling fractional reserve banking.

In 1811, with the 20-year charter about to expire, Congress

failed to renew it and the first Bank of the U.S. passed into
history with the sale of its assets to Stephen Gerard, a
Philadelphia financier.

Fast on the heels of the demise of the Bank of the U.S. came
the War of 1812 with a ruinous inflation fueled by the state
banks' issuance of credit in large multiples of their capital
reserves—since the only effective control over fractional reserve
issuance of notes died with the Bank of the U.S.

By 1816 the need for a central bank was again recognized and
a second Bank of the U.S. was established by Congress in much
the same form as the first Bank. It, too, was short-lived.
Criticism of the second Bank was identical to that of the first,
but by this time the number of its most fierce opponents, the
state banks, had grown to over 200. An attempt by Congress to
renew the charter of the second Bank of the U.S. was vetoed by
President Andrew Jackson and once again the country was
without a central bank.

There followed an era of frenzied growth and failure of state
banks during a period which lasted until 1864. Since the notes of
the state banks were not backed by the faith and credit of either
the U.S. Government or the state, each time a bank
failed, the losers were the people who held the bank note
(which were the main currency of the day). Overnight, the paper
became worthless.

You may ask, "What has this all got to do with making
money multiply, or building an estate?" In answer, a knowledge
of the operation of credit based on fractional reserves will give
you an insight into the causes and the possible cures for inflation, and provide a better understanding of money-making
strategies outlined in previous chapters. I mentioned earlier that
many people earned 19% on their money the first year and 25%
thereafter, with investments underwritten by agencies of the
U.S. Government. They recognized this opportunity because of

Figure 8. Obsolete (worthless) Bank Notes—
   Top: $1.00, Bank of Missouri, 1818.
   Bottom: $3.00, State Bank, Kansas Territory, 1856.

an understanding of fractional reserve credit and "float." So let's devote a bit more attention to bringing the history of American banking to modern times, to help you understand the present-day regulations that make it possible to earn interest on money before you have it, after you've spent it, and possibly on money you never did or will have.

The chaotic state banking system prevailed until the passage of the National Currency Act in 1864, which created the office of the Comptroller of the Currency and a system of national banks with regulations covering the capital, notes, reserve requirements, and loans.

Initially, on the surface, the state banks were not directly affected by the national banking system. However, the standing of notes issued by national banks rose so high relative to those of state banks that in short order people refused to accept state bank notes unless they were discounted—offered at a price below face value. The following year, in 1865, a federal tax of 10% was levied on state bank notes, a tax which caused the state bank notes to disappear from circulation. The complete demise of state banks was prevented by the growing use of checking accounts, which required no issuance of notes. And state banks could—and some did—obtain federal charters, thereby becoming members of the national system. However, many preferred to remain under the more lenient state control, rather than accept the stricter controls and limitations of the National Currency Act.

Among the many restrictions imposed upon the members of the national banking system were the following:

1. Minimum capital was specified, depending on the population of the city served.

2. A bank could not commence business until half the capital was paid in. The balance of the capital had to be paid in ensuing monthly installments of 10% each.

3. A portion of net earnings had to be retained until a surplus amounting to 20% of capital had been accumulated.

4. Each bank was required to deposit with the Comptroller of the Currency government bonds equal in amount to one-third of its capital, with a minimum of $30,000. The banks

were permitted to issue notes (obtained from the Comptroller) at first up to 90% and later 100% of the par value of the bonds. Additional notes could be issued only upon the deposit of additional bonds, but the total amount of notes issued by a bank could not exceed the bank's capital. In addition, there was an overall ceiling of $300 million on the total note issues of all national banks combined.

Reserve requirements were somewhat complex as a result of the practice of maintaining balances with correspondent banks. Banks customarily thought of these balances as part of their reserves, a practice which was continued under the national banking system.

Initially the reserve requirements of the act were applied to both note issues and loans, but as national bank notes circulated at par and proved to be readily redeemable, reserve requirements for note issues were eventually dropped.

The reserve that a large city bank had to keep (in lawful money such as standard money or government credit money) amounted to 25% of deposits; half in its vaults and the other half in correspondent banks. Balances in correspondent banks earned interest and drafts against them could be sold. Thus, although the reserve restrictions were superior to any previously required, they were not particularly prohibitive. In the case of rural banks, reserve requirements were even less restrictive.

The effect of the National Currency Act, which created the national banking system, was to establish a predominantly commercial banking system featuring a uniform code of operation.

From 1864 until 1913, with the passage of the Federal Reserve Act, both state and national banks continued to grow in number, until by the latter date there were about twice as many state as national banks. However, the national banks were usually large city banks, while state banks had limited resources, so that in reality national and state banks were of about equal importance.

Figure 9. $10 Note, National Bank of Charleston, Mass., 1875.

The inauguration of the national banking system was a decided step forward in that it provided complete safety for the circulating notes. A holder of a national bank note could not lose even if the issuing bank failed because the Treasury guaranteed the note and reimbursed itself by selling the deposited security. However, serious problems arose to demonstrate that the national banking system was not a cure-all.

One of the more obvious but less serious defects of the national banking system was the inadequate means of handling the nationwide clearing of checks, since the widespread use of checks was then in its early stage of development.

The clearing-house principle as applied to banking means simply that the banks in a community send checks drawn on other local banks to a central clearing house, rather than to each bank separately. There the checks are exchanged, or cleared, and only the net difference need be settled with each individual bank.

Under the national banking system, although the collecting of checks drawn on local banks presented no problem, the arrangement for collecting out-of-town checks was inadequate. The closest approach to a collection system was the use of the correspondent bank. This procedure not only delayed payment or crediting of checks but, due to the expense involved, also caused the face value of checks to be somewhat discounted, a factor which introduced uncertainty as to the true value of a check received. There was also a tendency for depositors to draw checks which would not be charged to their accounts for a considerable period of time, often several weeks, thereby leading to excesses in the use of existing deposits, in effect permitting a short-term fractional reserve system to be created by these depositors for themselves. (This should be remembered because it can still be accomplished today, to the profit of the depositor.)

Also, the system created the impression that the banks had greater reserves than they actually possessed since the receipt of a credit for the amount of a check at its correspondent bank was considered part of a bank's reserves. But when that correspondent bank in turn received credit for that same amount at *its* correspondent, it likewise counted the amount as reserves. (A variation on this theme permits an individual to earn interest at two banks at the same time on the same money.)

A more fundamental but less obvious defect concerned the issuing of national bank notes, which were still an important part of the total supply of money. Although the bond-secured currency system was a decided improvement over the excessive note issues of the state banks, the improvement was confined to the safety feature. Shortly, it was apparent that the currency system lacked the characteristic of "elasticity."

At certain times more money is needed by business to carry on transactions than at other times. This need varies from season to season, and from periods of prosperity to periods of reduced business activity. Businessmen need more money with which to meet their bills while goods are being produced, less money when the goods are sold. Farmers require extra funds for planting in the spring or harvesting in the fall, less after the crops are sold. At times of money need, businessmen and farmers would withdraw currency from banks and borrow additional funds, which they took from the banks in the form of deposits (to their accounts) or in currency.

But the national bank note issues were not designed to be elastic, that is, to expand and contract with the demand for money. In the first place, banks could not issue notes in an amount greater than their capital. Secondly, the amount of notes issued could not exceed the amount of the government bonds deposited as security for them. These limits were not related to the activities of business and therefore caused monetary scarcities in times of monetary need.

When withdrawals of currency exhausted the capacity of the banks to issue notes, it was necessary for them to pay out other forms of currency, such as United States notes or standard money which, in fact, were the banks' reserves. This reduced the banks' capacity to make loans at the very times when additional loans were needed. Consequently, not only were the note issues inelastic, but bank credit in general was inelastic—and worse, perversely elastic, since banks lost reserves when currency was withdrawn, and credit availability was *reduced* at the very time it was most needed.

The inability of banks to increase their available reserves was heightened at times because part of their reserves were maintained in the form of correspondent bank balances. Rural banks could count their balances in banks located in reserve or central cities as part of their reserves, and banks in reserve cities could count balances in central reserve city banks as one-half of their reserves. Therefore, banks in all parts of the country kept part of their reserves in the money centers, principally New York.

Like any other deposits in the New York banks, these balances were one of the banks' sources of funds. Thus, the New York banks were anxious to receive deposits from out-of-town banks in order to obtain loanable funds. Anticipating that the rural banks might wish to withdraw a large part of these funds to meet their seasonal needs for currency, the New York banks usually invested the funds in very liquid assets. Nevertheless, at times they were unable to meet the withdrawal demands of their rural bank customers.

The New York banks made loans to securities brokers as a means of employing these funds because brokerage loans, being callable, were supposedly very liquid. For example, a city bank receiving a deposit from a country bank might lend 75% of the amount to a broker and retain 25% as a cash reserve. Since the bank could call the loan at any time, it seemingly would be able to repay the deposit at any time. However, bank loans have a tendency to expand (the general principle of the expansion of bank loans) so that this broker's loan would lead to deposits at other New York banks, which in turn would expand their loans. Thus, the volume of brokers' loans might well be larger than the deposits of the rural banks.

What would happen if all the New York banks called all the brokers' loans at the same time? If one bank called its loans, the brokers could repay the loans by borrowing from other banks; but if all banks called the brokers' loans at the same time, the brokers could not repay because loans from other banks would be unavailable. The brokers would then be forced to sell the securities that were bought with the borrowed money. But who could buy the securities? Potential buyers likewise could not obtain bank funds. Funds with which to liquidate the brokers' loans simply would not exist.

It couldn't happen? It did—in 1873, 1893, and 1907. In these three years the banking system experienced what are called monetary panics; banks were unable to meet legitimate demands for loans and many businesses failed because of their inability to raise funds to pay their bills. At these times, the New York banks paid what they could to their rural customers, but were unable to raise enough money to meet the needs of the rural banks for currency. In 1873, the banks paid out funds in such large amounts that their reserves fell below the 25% requirement; hence they were barred from making loans until their reserves again exceeded 25% of deposits. In subsequent panics, banks suspended payments when reserves fell to the 25% level, and the securities markets plummeted, creating widespread losses.

At this point, think for a moment about what happened, albeit on a much smaller scale, when the Federal Reserve "tightened" money, creating the "credit crunch" of 1965. Interest rates skyrocketed; small businesses found bank loans unavailable; bills could not be paid and hundreds of sound small firms went bankrupt for want of bank credit.

Also, consider what might happen if any major percentage of the populace went to the banks to withdraw their savings. Don't for a moment believe that the limited resources of the Federal Deposit Insurance Corp. and the Federal Savings & Loan Insurance Corp. could prevent a panic of far greater magnitude than those of 1873, 1893, and 1907.

The development of the Federal Reserve System grew out of a need to remedy the inelasticity of the credit base of the country under the national banking system, while the later advent of the Federal Deposit Insurance Corp. came about because of the need to prevent bank failures due to panic demand for currency.

Since its inception during the depression years of the 30s, the Federal Deposit Insurance Corp. and its counterpart in the savings and loan industry, the Federal Savings & Loan Insurance Corp., have enjoyed the confidence of the public for the safety of their savings insured by these government agencies. Although there have been many bank and S & L failures, no one has ever yet lost a penny of funds insured by either the F.D.I.C. or the F.S.L.I.C.

However, it should be recognized that deposit insurance

would be unable to meet a sudden nationwide demand for currency actuated by some severe economic crisis. The depositor in an individual bank that fails is protected, provided that a great number of banks are not in a similar situation simultaneously.

A pound of gold would buy about the same amount of food, clothing, shelter, newspapers, oil, and coffee in 1932 as it does 47 years later. But it takes more than 10 times as many dollars. In terms of "standard money," that is, gold and silver, our currency, as well as most foreign monies, have been *devalued* by about 90%—and that in a period equivalent to the working lifetime of the average person.

So, although money must still be accepted as a medium of exchange, it is no longer a lasting standard of worth. It is, however, a commodity, to be "bought" and "sold." Unfortunately, it is a commodity that has consistently declined in value.

Although it may not be the most exciting reading, it is important that the reader learn about the evolution of the banking system—and how it works today—in order to attain the depth of understanding needed to take maximum advantage of its money-making potential.

C. The Federal Reserve System

Shortcomings in the structure, function, and operation of the national banking system gave rise to the establishment of the Federal Reserve System. Under the terms of the Federal Reserve Act of 1913, 12 regional central Federal Reserve Banks (FRBs) were established the following year. Banks that became "members" of the Federal Reserve System, were to utilize these central banks as repositories for part of the reserves that the member banks were required to maintain.

All national banks are required to belong to the Federal Reserve System, and state banks can become members by making application to the Board of Governors of the Federal Reserve System.

Although less than half of all banks in the U.S. are member banks, they have held three-quarters of the total amount of bank deposits, including both demand (check) and time (savings) deposits. Therefore, the Federal Reserve System is the dominant factor in American banking. Of the 8,000-odd non-member banks, the great majority are insured by the F.D.I.C., which makes them subject to the rules, regulations, and policies of that organization which, by design or accident, usually has a mutuality of interest with the Federal Reserve System. Although the member banks own the capital stock of the 12 regional Federal Reserve Banks, they own the reserve banks in name only, since the stock owners can neither exercise control over, nor determine policy of, the regional banks.

Each member bank must purchase an amount of capital stock of its regional Federal Reserve Bank equivalent to 3% of its capital and surplus. Each member can be required to purchase a like amount of stock in addition, but to date this requirement has not been exercised. The member banks all have a voice in the election of directors of the regional reserve banks and receive cumulative dividends of 6% on the capital stock of the reserve banks. Each of the 12 regional reserve banks are subject to the National Bank Act, the Federal Reserve Act, and the various regulations promulgated under these acts as supervised and directed by the Board of Governors of the Federal Reserve System. Although privately owned, the reserve banks operate as non-political, publicly oriented subsidiaries of the Federal Reserve System.

One of the most important innovations of the Federal Reserve is the ability of member banks to borrow from the regional reserve banks, thereby obtaining additional reserves when needed, as well as having an immediate source of currency when cash demand exceeds monetary supply. As a practical consequence, member banks utilize the reserve banks as a clearing-house for checks. As part of the price that banks pay to be members, they are subject to control by Federal Reserve Banks over general credit situations, through powers that may be exercised at the discretion and initiative of the reserve banks.

So that the Federal Reserve System might best serve the great areas and diverse resources of the entire country, the Federal Reserve Act provided for the division of the system into 12 districts, with each district having one regional reserve bank, and in most cases, branches.

1. Federal Reserve Bank of Boston

2. Federal Reserve Bank of New York, branch at Buffalo, N.Y.

3. Federal Reserve Bank of Philadelphia

4. Federal Reserve Bank of Cleveland, branches at Cincinnati, Ohio; Pittsburgh, Pa.

5. Federal Reserve Bank of Richmond, branches at Baltimore, Md.; Charlotte, N.C.

6. Federal Reserve Bank of Atlanta, branches at Birmingham, Ala.; Jacksonville, Fla.; Nashville, Tenn.; New Orleans, La.

7. Federal Reserve Bank of Chicago, branch at Detroit, Mich.

8. Federal Reserve Bank of St. Louis, branches at Little Rock, Ark.; Louisville, Ky.; Memphis, Tenn.

9. Federal Reserve Bank of Minneapolis, branch at Helena, Mont.

10. Federal Reserve Bank of Kansas City, Mo., branches at Denver, Colo.; Oklahoma City, Okla.; Omaha, Nebr.

11. Federal Reserve Bank of Dallas, branches at El Paso, Texas; Houston, Texas; San Antonio, Texas

12. Federal Reserve Bank of San Francisco, branches at Los Angeles, Cal.; Portland, Ore.; Salt Lake City, Utah; Seattle, Wash.

Since the policies of all of the reserve banks are subject to the direction of the Board of Governors of the Federal Reserve System, the effect is generally similar to what it would be were there one single central bank. However, decentralization is an important characteristic of the system at the operational level. Each reserve bank and each branch is a regional and local institution as well as part of a nationwide system; its transactions are with regional and local banks and businesses. It gives representation to the interests of its individual region and locale, while at the same time administering nationwide banking and credit policies. Thus, each reserve bank and branch enjoys some autonomy, subject only to the central system's policies.

As a central banking institution, the Federal Reserve System is not operated for profit, but rather in the public interest as decided by its Board of Governors.

Each of the 12 reserve banks is governed by a board of directors, representing various economic interests. There are three directors in each of three classes (A, B, and C), to a total of nine. The small member banks, medium-size banks, and large banks each elect one Class A and one Class B director. Class A directors are bankers while Class B directors are men actively engaged in industry, commerce, or agriculture within the district, but not actively associated with banks. The remaining three of the total nine, the Class C directors, are appointed by the Board of Governors of the Federal Reserve System from among business and professional men in the district who are not connected with banks. The Board of Governors selects one of its three choices to act as chairman of the board of directors of each of the reserve banks and as Federal Reserve Agent. Each of the branches has its own board of directors, with a majority of the directors appointed by the board of the reserve bank and a minority appointed by the Board of Governors of the FRB.

Though each of the reserve banks may exercise some flexibility in dealing with local problems, overall credit policies are controlled by the Board of Governors, which also retains the right of approval over the selection of various officials of each of the reserve banks, including presidents, first vice presidents, and vice presidents for research and for examinations.

Earnings of the reserve banks have decreased in importance, being controlled less by operations and more by credit policy. In the early years of the Fed (as the Federal Reserve is often referred to), earnings in excess of the dividend paid to stockholder members were divided between payment of a franchise tax and contributions to surplus. In order to increase the capital resources of the system, Congress repealed the franchise tax. During World War II, the Reserve System bought tremendous volumes of government bonds which yielded such great profits that the Board of Governors elected to turn over to the U.S. Treasury 90% of earnings in excess of expenses and dividends, with payments to the Treasury reaching close to a billion dollars a year.

At the apex of the Federal Reserve System is the seven-member Board of Governors, each member appointed by the President of the United States with the consent of the Senate for a term of 14 years. Every two years the term of one member expires, and a successor is appointed, thus creating stability and continuity minimally affected by political change. The Chairman and Vice Chairman are chosen by the President.

From their headquarters in the Federal Reserve Building in

Washington, D.C., the Board of Governors directs the operations and policies of the 12 reserve banks and their branches, and approves or establishes interest rates charged by reserve banks for advances (or loans) to member banks.

Policies relating to the buying and selling of government securities on the open market directly affect the amount of bank credit available to the general economy. Open market operations are run by the Federal Open Market Committee which is comprised of the seven governors plus the presidents of five of the reserve banks. The presidents of the 12 reserve banks take turns filling the five positions on the Open Market Committee.

The board of directors of each of the 12 reserve banks elects one member from their reserve district to sit on the Federal Advisory Council, which meets quarterly to confer with the Board of Governors on business and banking conditions prevailing in each of the areas of the country and to make advisory recommendations to the Board. In addition, to promote harmony and an understanding of individual and common problems confronting each of the reserve banks as well as the Board, the presidents of the 12 Federal Reserve Banks meet frequently with the Board of Governors.

Ostensibly to help insure the stability of member banks they supervise, and to strengthen their ability and power to control credit, the Board of Governors has been granted the power to control and set maximum interest rates allowed to be paid by member banks to depositors for savings and time deposits.

Federal Reserve officers wear four hats. Their mandate requires that the Fed act as a bank for banks, serve as the government's bank, supervise member banks to preserve their integrity, and manage the nation's money supply.

When business needs money, it is borrowed from a bank. Likewise, when a member bank needs money, it is borrowed from its district reserve bank.

The original national banking system had no power or ability to provide additional funds to the banking system when the need arose. In the old system the depository or correspondent banks in the central cities were privately owned, profit-making central banks. To maximize profits, they loaned funds to the limit of available reserves. Consequently, when country banks were in need of funds, they could be accommodated only if the depository or central bank liquidated part of its own loan portfolio. As private enterprise is in business for profit, the old central banks could not be expected to hold large sums idle to act as a safety valve or reservoir in times of money need.

Nor could the correspondent banks create reserves in excess of what they actually had when the need for such reserves was greatest. Rural banks had been permitted to consider their correspondent bank balances as part of their reserves, and therefore might have increased their reserve balances by borrowing from the correspondent bank, were it not that at the very time that many of the country banks wanted to borrow funds, the correspondent or city banks were themselves short of funds and unable to make loans to anyone, including the country banks.

The Federal Reserve System corrected this shortcoming. The new system permitted the reserve banks to create additional reserves as needed to make loans to member banks.

Member banks obtain their funds from their depositors, and the public uses demand deposits to satisfy its need for cash. Checks are the common instrument used for the withdrawal of demand deposits. If a bank receives more withdrawal checks than new deposits, it causes a decline in the bank's reserve balance as withdrawals are paid out in the form of Federal Reserve Notes (dollar bills) which become part of the currency in general circulation. However, when a bank grants loans, it is accomplished through the mechanism of creating a deposit for the borrower. Against this deposit, the borrower may draw funds (in the form of checks) as needed. Therefore, bank deposits are expanded (increased) when loans are granted.

By the same reasoning, an expansion of the obligations of a central bank creates more funds that can be used as bank reserves. In consequence, reserve banks make loans to member banks by means of the discount process (see page 208) and, since the additional sums are credited to the member banks' reserve balances, a loan from the reserve banks adds to the available supply of bank reserves.

If this explanation sounds like double-talk, as it probably does to the non-banker, it may be made understandable if one considers that a central bank bears the same relationship to its member banks as a commercial bank bears to the public. Its obligations are deposits and notes, and these are used as money or currency. If the term "note" is confusing, examine the dollar bill. Imprinted at the top is "Federal Reserve Note" and the phrase "This note is legal tender for all debts, public and private." This dollar bill or Federal Reserve Note is merely evidence of an obligation of Federal Reserve to the note holder.

At one time, as mentioned previously, notes or currency were measured against some arbitrary standard such as gold or silver so that their value would be assured. Today it is only a medium of exchange backed by confidence—which may well be misplaced when we witness its constantly declining value.

While notes are used as currency by the public, deposits are used between banks. As reserve requirement regulations limit the expansion of deposits by member banks, so the central bank had been limited in deposit expansion by such restraints as the requirement of gold reserve maintenance.

Control over bank reserve requirements is an effective tool in controlling economic activity. At first, the Federal Reserve Act only required member banks to keep part of their reserves as balances in the reserve banks. During World War I, the Act was amended so that all required reserves of member banks had to be kept in the reserve banks. In 1935, the Board of Governors of the Federal Reserve were authorized to increase reserve requirements up to double those previously provided for in the Act, and in 1960 the cash that member banks kept in their vaults was again permitted to be counted as part of their legal reserves.

The reserve banks were in a position to make loans when member banks purchased stock and made deposits into the reserve bank. However, the reserve banks were not established to operate at a profit, or to compete with their member banks, but rather to act as a safety valve and reservoir of funds for the banks. It is the responsibility of the reserve banks to advance or loan funds to member banks when the economy's borrowing need is greater than the member banks can themselves fulfill. In this way business activity can be maintained at high levels. Conversely, when the Fed decides to slow down the economy, it need merely decrease the amount of money available to member banks from the reserve banks, or increase the cost of that money, or both.

To protect the System from the banks, and to protect the banks from themselves—lest member banks borrow money indiscriminately from the reserve banks—some guidelines were established. To obtain loans from the reserve banks, member banks had to put up what is termed "eligible paper," evidence of short-term obligations drawn to finance actual business or agricultural transactions. Some time after the inception of the Federal Reserve, U.S. Government obligations were added to the list of eligible paper.

Prior to 1935, the Federal Reserve Act defined eligible paper as notes, acceptances, or bills of exchange arising out of commercial transactions, provided that such paper matured in less than 91 days, except for agricultural paper which was permitted maturities up to nine months. Loans made to finance the purchase of stocks or bonds, except for U.S. Government securities, were not classed as eligible paper. In 1935 the Act was amended to permit advances or loans from reserve banks to member banks on their time or demand notes with maturities of four months or less, provided that the notes were secured to the satisfaction of the reserve bank. Such loans, made on the security of what was called "acceptable paper" as compared to eligible paper, required the payment of interest rates one-half per cent higher than the rate charged for loans made against eligible paper.

Of course, whereas reserve banks are supposed to be operated in the public interest, the member banks are strictly private enterprise in business for profit. It follows, and experience has revealed, that member banks made a profusion of loans during good times, when eligible paper was readily available, while in bad times, when eligible paper was scarce, banks made far too few loans. Since one of the concepts behind the Federal Reserve System was that of making money (as loans) available in bad times to stimulate the economy, modifications of the Reserve Act were indicated and have been made gradually.

Originally, the actual operation of borrowing from Federal Reserve Banks did not conform to theory or expectations. Banks made loans to customers by discounting, advancing (for example) $9,900 to the customer in exchange for a $10,000 promissory note due and payable in 60 days. As a bank made many similar discount loans, it gradually reduced its reserves (as the borrowers withdrew the loaned funds from their accounts). Eventually, during times of great loan activity, bank reserves were depleted to such an extent that its required reserve ratio no longer permitted additional loans to be made. However, since this type of discount note was eligible paper, the member bank could rediscount this note at the reserve bank to replenish its monetary supply. Gradually, the practice of rediscounting notes gave way to discounting; the reserve bank made loans against the member bank's own note, secured by eligible or acceptable paper, rather than directly against the eligible or acceptable paper. The only real difference between discounting and rediscounting is the mechanics; the end result is the same.

The operations of the reserve system were meant to be almost automatic. Existence of eligible paper proved that banks were making loans to meet economic need. It was thus expected that reserves in the form of balances at the reserve banks would expand or contract in proportion to the needs of the business community for financing. As demand for loans waned, loans would be repaid at a faster rate than new loans were made; loan or deposit levels would fall, and the ratio of reserves to loans (or deposits) would rise. Since additional reserves would no longer be necessary (loan demand having waned), rediscounting of paper would be reduced. This principle was labeled "elasticity" by economists; bank credit was supposed to expand and contract according to the needs of the economy.

However, the system had not reckoned with the hoarding of currency due to a loss of confidence in banks, as became widespread during the early years of the great depression. At that time, business borrowing was at a very low level, and banks had to deplete reserve balances in order to satisfy the demand for currency. But the banks had only a small amount of eligible paper available for rediscounting at the reserve banks, since loan activity was at a low level. Elasticity was shown not to be the cure-all. Funds available from reserve banks for member banks through rediscounting of eligible paper were insufficient to meet the cash withdrawal or hoarding demand. To save the banking system from widespread failures, the reserve banks, by authority of the 1935 amendment to the Federal Reserve Act, made advances to member banks on "acceptable" paper (loans of less than four months' duration, such as those made to finance the purchase of stocks or bonds).

The volume of bank reserves is affected by the reserve banks' power to make discounts and advances. Bank reserves are also affected by open market operations, which are under the direction of the Federal Open Market Committee, an arm of the Federal Reserve System. When the Federal Reserve Bank purchases government securities, reserves are increased; when it sells, reserves are decreased. The Federal Reserve Bank of New York acts as agent for the Federal Open Market Committee in the execution of transactions. Put simply, if the Fed purchases securities from a member bank (acting as a dealer), the reserve account of the member bank is credited. If the Fed sells securities to or through a member bank, the member bank's reserve account is debited. Thus, the Federal Reserve System can increase or decrease the total volume of member banks' reserves by buying or selling securities on the open market.

In contrast, the Board of Governors' power to increase or decrease reserve *requirements* does not increase or decrease actual reserves, although the effect of such actions on the economy is similar to the effect of decreasing or increasing actual reserves, as is accomplished by buying or selling of securities by the Fed.

Control over the availability of bank credit is easily exercised by the Board of Governors through increasing or decreasing reserve requirements. As an example, assume that the actual combined reserves of all member banks average 15% at a time when member banks are required to maintain a minimum of 10% in reserves. Loans from member banks would be readily available, or, so to speak, money would be loose, because one-third of the banks' reserves, or 5%, are excess reserves which the member banks may use to increase loans and investments. However, if the Board decides that economic activity should be slowed down, the Board could raise the reserve requirements from 10% to 15%, thereby automatically converting the excess reserves into required reserves. At this point, the only ways that banks could make new loans would be by selling some of their own investments or securities, or by discounting at the reserve bank. To discourage the latter, discounting, all the reserve bank need do is raise the discount rate. In addition, credit can be tightened even more if the Fed, through its Open Market Committee, either stops purchasing, or actually sells government securities, the latter course creating a diminution of member banks' reserves.

The tremendous power that this seven-member Board of Governors wields over banks, business, and the public welfare is obvious; it is subject only to the restraints of conscience and

judgment, and the ability of the Congress to amend the Federal
Reserve Act.

Another responsibility of the Federal Reserve System is that
of keeping the nation supplied with currency. Except for early
issues of Federal Reserve Bank Notes, Federal Reserve Notes
are the dominant currency. The so-called dollar bill is actually a
note evidencing the indebtedness by the Federal Reserve to the
holder, a note that is sanctioned as legal tender for the payment
of all debts. This note does not assure any real value; it cannot
be exchanged for a fixed amount of precious metal, or anything
else. Its value is only what it will buy in the market place. Thus,
of no intrinsic value, its worth lies in the confidence of its
holders that it will have enduring value in the market place. The
endurance of its worth perhaps can be measured by a simple
yardstick: About 25 years ago the $10 Federal Reserve Note
bought 75 copies of the Sunday *Times plus* 50 rides on the New
York City subway. Today that $10 note buys 10 copies of that
newspaper and three rides on the subway.

In conformity with the basic concept of the Federal Reserve
System, currency, in the form of Federal Reserve Notes, was
designed to be elastic, just as was bank credit. As depositors
made withdrawals in currency from banks, the Federal Reserve
Banks issued Federal Reserve Notes when and as needed, and
maintained only a fractional gold reserve plus a cover of collateral in the form of eligible paper. Therefore, when an increase in reserves was made necessary by an increase in loan or
currency-withdrawal demand, member banks rediscounted
eligible paper with the reserve banks, thereby providing the
reserve banks with collateral or cover for issuing additional currency as Federal Reserve Notes. At the other end of the cycle,
when the currency was returned to the banks in repayment of
loans or as deposits, the banks used the currency notes to reim-
burse the reserve banks for their indebtedness. Thus, currency
issues expanded and contracted as needed, as did credit; the
principle of elasticity encompassed credit, legal reserves, and
currency.

Since all member banks maintain reserve balances at their reserve banks, the operation of the Federal Reserve System presented an opportunity to establish an efficient check collection and clearing system. In addition to member banks, non-member banks participate in the Fed's check clearing system by maintaining clearing balances to assure payment at reserve banks. (Clearing balances required of non-member banks by the Fed are analogous to deposits required by public utilities of their customers.)

With checks both drawn on and deposited into banks served by the same Federal Reserve Bank, the reserves of the paying bank are charged while the receiving bank is credited with the amount of the check. When a check drawn on a bank served by one reserve bank is deposited into a bank served by another reserve bank, the latter bank sends the check to its own reserve bank for collection. The reserve bank credits the amount of the check to the reserve account of the bank that sent them the check, and sends the check to the reserve bank that serves the bank upon which the check was drawn. This reserve bank then debits the reserve account of the paying bank. Thus, if a thousand dollar check is drawn against an account in the ABC Bank in California and is deposited by the recipient into his account in the XYZ Bank in New York, the XYZ Bank will send the check to the Federal Reserve Bank in N.Y., where the reserve account of the XYZ Bank will be credited with $1,000. Meanwhile, the Reserve Bank in N.Y. sends the check to the Federal Reserve Bank of San Francisco (or one of its branches that may be serving the ABC Bank), where the reserve account of the ABC Bank is debited by $1,000. The example demonstrates the time-consuming handling that is required in the check clearing process.

> With automation, magnetic scanning, and the increased use of computers, it is expected that eventually check clearing as well as the adjustment of reserve balances will be almost instantaneous. As it is, the Fed has reduced clearance time for the check-depositing bank to a maximum of two days from the time the reserve bank receives a check.

From the time a check is written to the time the amount of the check is deducted from the check writer's account is the period when a check is "floating" in limbo. As we have seen, until the time when check clearing, crediting, and debiting becomes instantaneous, the limbo period, called "float," can be a profitable tool for the bank customer or business firm smart enough to take advantage of it.

Regardless of the time required for the clearing process, banks lose reserves to the amount that checks are drawn on them, and gain reserves to the amount that checks are deposited into them. Likewise, when banks make loans, the loaned sum is deposited to the borrower's account, but as the borrower withdraws funds from his account (by writing checks drawn on his account in the bank) the bank loses reserves as these drawn checks clear.

It can be seen that bank reserves can fluctuate markedly from day to day. Because of this fluctuation, reserve requirements stipulated by the Fed for member banks are based on average reserves, weekly in the case of banks located in reserve cities, biweekly for country banks.

Transactions among Federal Reserve Banks are handled through the Interdistrict Settlement Fund in the Federal Building in Washington, D.C. At the close of business each day, each of the reserve banks wires the clearing agent of the Board of Governors citing the total amount that reserve bank owes to each of the other reserve banks as a result of the check clearing process. The account of each reserve bank is debited with the sum it owes the other reserve banks, and is credited with the amounts owed to it by each of the other reserve banks. The result is either a net debit or a net credit to the settlement fund account of each reserve bank.

To insure that member banks maintain their integrity, remain a safe depository for the public's funds, abide by the multitude of regulations imposed by the Fed and do not engage in corrupt practices, all member banks are subjected to audits at least annually. National Banks are audited by the office of the Comptroller of the Currency, while all other member banks are audited by a staff of examiners in the employ of the Federal Reserve System.

We have seen that each of the reserve banks has as customers the member banks in their respective districts. The Fed in Washington acts as a bank for its 12 district banks plus one retail customer, the United States Government. Just as a neighborhood bank keeps your checking account and lends you money on your I.O.U., so the Federal Reserve handles the account of the government.

It was mentioned before that the Fed has four jobs to do: act as a bank for banks; function as the government's bank; supervise member banks to preserve their safety and honesty; and manage the nation's money supply.

The history of the System shows that it has performed remarkably efficiently in doing the first two jobs. Despite a number of member-bank failures due to corruption or malfeasance, a good job has also been done with their third responsibility. How well the Federal Reserve System, through its Board of Governors, has performed in their fourth task, that of managing money, would be an interesting subject for debate.

D. The People Banks

In addition to the commercial banking system, the savings banks and the savings and loan associations should be of major interest to those who would maximize the return on their savings.

Savings banks, especially the mutual savings banks in New England and New York State, are well known as gatherers of relatively small savings which are invested in mortgage loans and conservative securities. State laws generally define the conservative nature of the loans and investments which mutual savings banks may make, while commercial banks are not as stringently limited.

The early part of the 19th Century saw the founding of many savings banks, the first two being in Philadelphia and Boston in 1816, for reasons that were largely philanthropic. These banks provided the means whereby small savings could be encouraged, so that the poor might accumulate funds as a bulwark against poverty. The gathered funds were placed in mortgages on all kinds of urban properties as well as farms, and invested in high grade government and corporate bonds.

This mutual form of bank organization did not spread to any large extent outside of the northeastern part of the country, where nearly all of the approximately 500 mutual savings banks are located. The conservative management policies of these banks and the nature of their investments brought them through the great depression of the 1930s without any formal failures, even though the collapse of mortgage values at that time did present serious problems. Nevertheless, the growth rate of deposits in mutual savings banks in the post-World War II period was slower than that of both time deposits (savings deposits) in commercial banks and shares (equivalent to savings deposits) in savings and loan associations.

It is of interest to note that the Federal Deposit Insurance Corporation has the authority to set maximum interest rates payable by either member commercial or savings banks on time deposits. Since all banks which are members of the Federal Reserve System are automatically covered by F.D.I.C. insurance, this quasi-private entity possesses and has exercised its power to establish and maintain a distinct inequity between interest rates that a commercial bank may pay out and that permitted to be paid by mutual savings banks.

This deliberate ordering of interest inequity between time deposits in savings banks and commercial banks—higher in the case of savings banks, ostensibly because of their more conservative investments—represents a policy decision to cause a forced flow of funds to savings banks in order to maintain a sizable source of low-cost money to be used for mortgage funds.

Given the capacity of commercial banks to earn and thereby to pay out higher interest rates than they are now permitted to pay, the deliberate policy of restricting interest rates by savings banks, and even lower rates by commercial banks, in effect obliges a large segment of the saving public to subsidize the private mortgage-money borrower. It is true that state laws limit the rate of interest that banks can charge the individual on a mortgage, but neither the states, the Federal Government, the Federal Reserve, nor the F.D.I.C. have limited the interest rates chargeable on loans or mortgages to corporate business. This being the case, banks put most of their money where it will earn the most—in loans and mortgages on business properties. And they make these loans with the money that the individual deposits into savings accounts at interest rates that are kept so low—by U.S. Government agency fiat—that not only does the depositor not increase the value of his savings, but actually suffers heavy losses because the interest paid on savings, particularly after payment of income taxes thereon, is not nearly sufficient to offset the erosion of value due to inflation. So, not only is the little guy forced to subsidize the private mortgage-money market, but also the banks—which take his money at controlled low-interest rates and lend out that money at uncontrolled high rates.

During the early 1800s, increasing numbers of people flocked to the cities. In those days, the usual depository for the meager savings of the working class was the cookie jar—or under the mattress. Commercial banks could not be bothered with the pennies, nickels, and dimes of the laborers, handling rather the financing of trade, shipping, and agriculture. Banks likewise did not accommodate the individual's need for home-building loans. At the time, mortgage loans were made almost exclusively by individuals, entrepreneurs, or loan sharks, and demand far exceeded the limited supply of such loans.

Since there were no banks that catered to the working class, either as a place in which to keep savings or from which to borrow, someone had to invent them—and did in 1816 when savings banks came into being. Eighteen hundred thirty one saw the founding of the first savings and loan association, while life insurance companies, which had existed since Colonial days, proliferated in number and expanded in assets.

Though their purposes, structure, and operations differ, these three types of organizations—savings banks, savings and loan associations, and life insurance companies—have two important characteristics in common: they issue amortizing home mortgages, and are a repository of savings in comparatively modest amounts.

Of the three, the savings and loan associations have always had as their prime objective the financing of private homes. They not only specialize in, but are required by law and regulations to confine their lending activities primarily to home mortgage financing.

The Philadelphia area, where Ben Franklin had organized a number of cooperative enterprises including the first mutual fire insurance company, witnessed the organization of the first association, the original cornerstone of the now giant savings and loan industry.

Forty people in the town of Frankford, a suburb of Philadelphia, in early 1831 formed the Oxford Provident Building Association, patterned after the building clubs and societies in England that had as their purpose the providing of home financing for their members. Each member of the Oxford Association paid an initiation fee of $5.00 and dues of $3.00 per month. As sufficient money accumulated in the association for a member to borrow, the funds would be advanced to him as a secured mortgage loan to be repaid in monthly installments with interest over a 10-year term. Unlike the savings and loan associations of today, the Oxford Association was not designed to operate in perpetuity, but rather to cease operations once all of its members had obtained homes.

In April of 1831, the town lamplighter, a man of modest means with the unlikely name of Comly Rich, was given the first amortizing mortgage loan, a sum of $375, for the purchase of a small cottage. Built on an 11 x 15-foot foundation, the house had a living room or parlor on the ground floor and a bedroom on each of the second and attic floors. Three years later, Comly Rich borrowed an additional $125 presumably to add a kitchen onto the ground floor. The original house, unchanged except for new clapboard installed at the front of the house, still stands today, a monument to the savings and loan industry.

In short order, other savings and loan associations sprang up under many names, including land or loan associations, building associations, building and loans, homestead associations, and cooperative banks, not only in the Philadelphia area, but across the entire country. Today, there are more than a million shareholders for every one who was a member of the pioneering Oxford Provident Building Association.

During this period of growth, associations underwent a metamorphosis. The original concept of a temporary local self-help society gradually changed to one of permanence, with the scope enlarged to include deposit and loan facilities for greater numbers of people. The functions of savings and borrowings separated; shareholder members were free to deposit for interest, with no obligation to borrow, while borrowers had no obligation to be depositors.

As more and more states chartered savings and loan associations, though methods of operation changed, basically the associations still offered fully amortizing mortgages as they had done since the first days of 1831—long before other lenders embraced the idea. Except for recent years, when stock-company savings and loan associations arose in a few states, most associations were mutually owned by depositors, as are the mutual savings banks.

During the almost sesquicentury history of American savings and loan associations, from the modest beginnings of the Oxford Provident Building Association with less than 40 members, the industry has grown to about two hundred billion dollars and a dozen million outstanding mortgages, the third largest financial type of institution in the United States, exceeded in assets only by commercial banks and life insurance companies.

Until a few years ago, deposits in savings and loan associations were not considered by the Internal Revenue Service to be the same as deposits in banks, but were the purchase of shares (securities), albeit securities that were exempt from certain regulations of the Securities and Exchange Commission.

The fact that most savings banks and savings and loan associations are mutually owned by depositors can be misleading to the unsophisticated. The individual depositor-"owner" has no more to say about the management of the institution and less to gain from its profits than the owner of one share of stock in a corporation. Entrenched management controls both corporations and mutual savings institutions. Bank and association profits are used to build magnificent new edifices, pay senior management's high salaries, and provide almost unlimited expense accounts in addition to extravagent fringe benefits—but not one cent of these profits go to the "owners" who must be satisfied with the meager interest per-

mitted to be paid to them "by law." At least in the case of
private (stockholder-owned) banks and associations, the stockholders have invested their money in order to own the stock,
while with those that are "mutual," the management, which
reaps much of the benefits, has not invested a cent in stock
ownership. If a private bank fails, the investors are the first and
principal losers; if a mutual bank fails, the losers are not the investors, because there are no investors, but rather the depositors
and (or) the public through the loss of government-agency
insurance funds. The early 19th Century mutual banks and
associations were truly mutual endeavors. (The present-day
ones might well be frauds perpetrated on a naive public.)

Index